★★ 2023-24 EDITION

Prepare for Social Security

THE INSIDER'S GUIDE™ TO MAXIMIZING YOUR RETIREMENT BENEFITS

Matt Feret

LOOKING FOR A TRUSTED ADVISOR?

Social Security and Medicare are closely related. Many readers have sought my personal recommendation for a dependable licensed insurance agent as described in my books. You know, the kind that avoids high-pressure sales, is unbiased in their advice, keeps in touch through the years, and truly aids in navigating the Medicare maze. There are probably agents like this in your hometown, but I certainly don't know all of them.

If you're looking for this kind of insurance agent, I've got the perfect person: my wife, Niki. Now, you might give me a funny look for me recommending my wife's agency, but the quality of the service I put my name behind means everything to me, and frankly, she's doing incredible work helping people. I'd recommend her even if I didn't promise to love, honor, and cherish.

Her agency can assist clients in all but a handful of states.

With almost ten years of experience as an independent insurance agent, she embodies the expertise and values I advocate. Niki heads the Brickhouse Agency - a boutique insurance firm. Representing only trusted and fully vetted carriers, her team provides guidance on Medicare insurance options. She also donates 10% of her firm's annual net profit to charity.

To discuss your Medicare needs or upcoming enrollment, you can:

— Book a complimentary consultation on the Prepare for Medicare website, or the Prepare for Social Security website. There is no obligation to enroll. There's also a chat function on each website, if you prefer to engage that way.

— Call (844) 844-6565 to schedule an appointment with a licensed insurance agent from her firm.

Most folks prefer a Zoom meeting (camera off is fine!), but a phone call can be scheduled, too. Niki's services are entirely free for clients. Any compensation her firm receives comes directly from the Medicare insurance companies. If you reach out, be sure to tell her I sent you!

Prepare for Social Security

THE INSIDER'S GUIDE™
TO MAXIMIZING YOUR RETIREMENT BENEFITS

Matt Feret

Copyright 2023 © Matt Feret/MF Media, LLC

All rights reserved. No part of this book may be reproduced or transmitted in any form or by any means, electronic or mechanical, including photocopying, recording, or by any information storage and retrieval system without written permission of the publisher, except for the inclusion of brief quotations in a review.

Hardcover ISBN: 979-8-9879933-0-9

Paperback ISBN: 979-8-9879933-1-6

eBook ISBN: 979-8-9879933-2-3

DISCLAIMER

This book is in no way associated with, endorsed, or authorized by the Social Security Administration, the Department of Health and Human Services, or the Centers for Medicare and Medicaid Services. This book is in no way sponsored, associated, authorized, approved, endorsed, nor in any way affiliated with any company, trademarked names, or other marks. Any such mention is for the purpose of reference only. Any advice, generalized statistics, or opinions expressed are strictly those of the author's. Although every effort has been made to ensure the contents of this book are correct and complete, Social Security and Medicare rules, premiums, and coverages change quickly and often. The book isn't meant to replace the sage advice of healthcare, insurance, financial planning, accounting, or legal professionals. You are responsible for your financial decisions. It is your sole responsibility to independently evaluate the accuracy, correctness, or completeness of the content, services, and products of, and associated with, this publication.

The thoughts and opinions expressed in this publication are those of the author only, and are not the thoughts and opinions of any current or former employer of the author. Nor is this publication made by, on behalf of, or endorsed or approved by any current or former employer of the author.

TABLE OF CONTENTS

INTRODUCTION i

CHAPTER ONE
WHAT IS SOCIAL SECURITY? 1

CHAPTER TWO
DECIDING WHEN TO FILE FOR SOCIAL SECURITY 22

CHAPTER THREE
SOCIAL SECURITY ELECTION CASE STUDIES 43

CHAPTER FOUR
THE "FRUSTRATING FLAWS" OF SOCIAL SECURITY 57

CHAPTER FIVE
THE SOCIAL SECURITY MARKETING MACHINE 68

CHAPTER SIX
UNDERSTANDING HOW SOCIAL SECURITY
AND MEDICARE WORK TOGETHER 79

CHAPTER SEVEN
FILING FOR SOCIAL SECURITY BENEFITS:
DIY (DO-IT-YOURSELF) 91

CHAPTER EIGHT
FILING FOR SOCIAL SECURITY BENEFITS:
HIRE A CONSULTANT OR ADVISOR 107

CHAPTER NINE
BRINGING IT ALL TOGETHER
AND FORMULATING YOUR PLAN 116

CHAPTER TEN
SPECIAL SITUATIONS: DIVORCE, DISABILITY,
CONTINUING TO WORK, AND MORE 125

ACKNOWLEDGEMENTS 137

GLOSSARY 138

WHO IS MATT FERET? 144

INDEX 146

SPECIAL INVITATION

Please note that Social Security rules, regulations, policies, and benefits are subject to change. If you'd like to get the most up-to-date information, find the nearest Social Security office near you, gain access to NSSA-Certified Social Security advisors, explore my online courses, view the "Helpful Links" section, sign up for my newsletter, or download free helpful checklists referenced in the book, join us at https://PrepareforSocialSecurity.com.

Hello, and thanks for reading this book! I'm Matt, and I like helping people. I write books, create courses, and host shows that address older adult, retirement, and caregiver issues.

Social Security and Medicare are closely related and I've worked in the Medicare insurance industry since 2001, and I still learn things every day about Medicare and Social Security. It doesn't matter if you have a GED or Ph.D, this stuff is confusing for everyone. These programs change constantly, and each year <u>both programs directly impact your finances.</u>

That's why I've created online courses and written about both topics in my books, *Prepare for Medicare – The Insider's Guide to Buying Medicare Insurance* and *Prepare for Social Security – The Insider's Guide to Maximizing Your Retirement Benefits.*

Speaking of my online courses, I created two websites chock-full of Medicare and Social Security-specific resources as compliments to both topics. You can enroll in my courses on either website, and if you need an experienced independent insurance agent, or highly qualified fee-only Social Security consultant, both sites connect you to fully vetted professionals I trust.

If you already have a Medicare insurance plan, it's not too late to ask for a review! Remember, it costs nothing and if you're not reviewing your Medicare coverage every year, you're probably paying too much! *(I only recommend products or services to our readers that I would recommend to my own family members. I only recommend products and services with businesses and/or individuals I have personally vetted or have a relationship with. None of them influence my editorial decisions.)*

You can find all of this at:

www.PrepareforMedicare.com

www.PrepareforSocialSecurity.com

Medicare and Social Security are both very important parts of your financial well-being, but they're not the be-all, end-all of a successful retirement. That's why I created and host my very own podcast and YouTube channel, The Matt Feret Show. The Matt Feret Show focuses on the health, wealth and wellness of adults, retirees, and caregivers helping loved ones. I interview interesting people, insiders, and experts to help light a path to successful living in midlife and beyond. I've been told my whole life I have the gift of gab, and I love nothing more than meeting and chatting with bright, fascinating people. So that's what my guests and I do on the podcast; offer a wealth of relevant, timely, and useful information through a friendly conversation. I'm confident you'll get as much out of listening to it as I do in making it. It's much more like listening to trusted friends talk about something that's important to you, too!

www.TheMattFeretShow.com

All three websites allow you to sign up for my FREE newsletter. When you do, you'll immediately get access to handy Medicare and Social Security checklists you can download, also for FREE—a gift for just signing up for my newsletter. No spam here (heck, I don't like that, either). I send a few a month, and cover useful, informative and actionable information covering Social Security, Medicare, and many other retirement topics that help you feel less confused, and more informed about these really important decisions you have to make.

In closing: here's to your wealth, wisdom and wellness!

—matt feret

Matt Feret

INTRODUCTION

YOU GET ONE SHOT TO MAKE YOUR DECISION

The vast majority of the decisions you make in life are not permanent. If you buy a house, you can always sell it and move. If you go into a certain career, you can always make an exit and train for another line of work. And if you get a tattoo—something that used to be seen as permanent—you can have it removed.

However, there are a few decisions that are permanent. You get one shot—one chance to make a decision.

Deciding when to take Social Security in retirement is one of those "do or die" moments. You get one chance to claim it and one chance to make it right, except for the one-time withdrawal of benefits described later in the book. Making the wrong choice can cost you tens of thousands (or even hundreds of thousands) of dollars. Even worse, it could cost your heirs over *their* lifetimes.

This all sounds harsh, but it's true. Even if you have a pension, insurance, or retirement accounts to supplement Social Security, it is still a significant chunk of income in your retirement years that you or your spouse earned—and are entitled to—over your lifetime.

Like other government programs, Social Security often gets a bad rap. Does it provide everything you would like? Probably not. Is the system complicated to navigate? Yes. Is there lots of conflicting advice out there to confuse you even more? Of course.

Even so, I'm here to help you navigate the complex and often befuddling world of Social Security. I also want to help you make the best decision possible about when to apply for benefits and how to maximize them.

In a nutshell, the purpose of Social Security is to supplement the income you lose when you retire or become disabled, or your dependents and survivors, if any, lose when you die. Except for disability, your monthly check near retirement, or while retired, is based on your 35 best years of earnings. While it's not 100% accurate, you can think of it as an insurance program or an annuity that provides income for the rest of your life. Your Social Security payments rise with inflation and, unlike most investments, are protected from the rise and fall of fluctuations in the stock and bond markets. If you are married, your spouse will continue to receive a portion of your benefits even when you die. Your payments are guaranteed for life.

It is easy to take Social Security for granted. But consider this: if you lived one hundred years ago, there was no guaranteed income in your retirement years except for what you might have saved or what your family could provide. When you look at it this way, you begin to realize there is a lot to love about Social Security!

As a retiree, the biggest danger you face is running out of savings because you can't accurately predict how long you will live. Social Security is designed to provide a predictable source of income regardless of how much you have (or don't have) in savings, investments, assets, or help from your family.

That's the good news. The bad news is that dealing with Social Security is a lot like buying a new computer. You're not a specialist. A lot of what you "know" you've simply "heard" from other people, AM radio hosts, and random people on YouTube and Facebook. I get it; a lot of what they've told you contradicts itself or just doesn't make sense. You know it's important, but you're nervous about messing it up and just don't want to have to think about it.

When you ask an expert for advice, what they say is full of technical jargon you don't really care about. And often, you find out the person giving you advice only wants to sell you something. You aren't looking for a salesman;

you're looking for someone who knows what they're talking about and genuinely wants to help you.

If that is true of a major purchase like a computer, it's even more true of your decision on Social Security. It's a once-in-a-lifetime decision that will affect your family's financial future for years to come, including your heirs'.

The system is complicated and confusing to navigate. To give you one example, in the case of married couples, the formula for determining each person's benefit consists of ten mathematical calculations. The Social Security Administration (SSA) personnel aren't much help, either. They are overloaded and are not equipped to give you the best advice for your specific situation. (Throughout the book, I will refer to the Social Security Administration as the SSA.)

Unlike Medicare, you only get one shot at deciding when to start taking Social Security. And unlike Medicare, your choice affects your spouse and potentially your children and heirs. Some people wait until they are 70 years old to claim their Social Security benefits, but the majority of people take it early at 62. Why? Because most people believe Social Security is going to go bankrupt or that they will die before they can maximize their benefits. Therefore, they take it too early, potentially costing themselves and their heirs many thousands of dollars.

Prepare for Social Security—The Insider's Guide will give you an insider's view of how to best choose when to start drawing Social Security benefits and how to navigate a system that is not easy to understand. Please note that because it is such a vast topic, we are focusing only on Social Security for retirees and will not go in-depth into Social Security for those on disability.

When it comes to reaping the benefits of all the years you have put into working, you don't want to make a critical mistake that could cost you a large chunk of your income. Remember—there is no magic answer to the question "When should I start claiming my Social Security benefits?" The answer depends on a variety of factors.

But there is no need to go it alone. I'm here to help save you time, reduce your frustration, and give you peace of mind as you consider your options. I am thrilled to be your guide on this journey to making one of the most critical decisions of your life.

A quick note about terminology before we move forward: you've probably noticed I have used the term "spouse" a few times already. In this book, we will use the term "spouse" instead of "partner" to ensure there is clarity. The SSA uses the term "spouse" to apply to legally married people. This applies to same-sex or opposite-sex couples. I will stick with the term "spouse" since that's the language used by the SSA (source: https://PrepareforSocialSecurity.com/sources).

THERE ARE USUALLY TWO TYPES OF SOCIAL SECURITY RECIPIENTS

1. People who like to do their own research and make the best decision. They want to know everything about the subject. They are skeptical of advisors and salespeople and like to DIY everything. (If this describes you, feel free to head straight for Chapter 7.)
2. People who don't like the hassle of having to learn everything about a topic. They just want a knowledgeable expert to tell them what to do. They don't want to deal with Social Security; they want someone to make it easy or secure the help of a qualified advisor or consultant. (If this describes you, head toward Chapter 8.)

No matter which category you fall into, this book is for you!

Please know there are no shortcuts or "hacks" when it comes to Social Security. There is no way of getting around the system, and it isn't wise to let someone else do all your decision-making. You need to have some measure of knowledge so you can make the wisest decision about Social Security because your future could quite literally depend on it.

However, there is no need to fear. Even though the system isn't *simple*, I'm here to *simplify* it. You'll learn the basics of Social Security, when to start claiming your benefits, how to avoid getting sucked into the Social Security marketing machine, whether to DIY or to get professional help, how to file, and much more.

If you read this book and follow my guidance, it shouldn't take you any more than a few hours. That's a tiny investment of time compared to the massive benefits you could see from making a wise, informed decision about Social Security.

Once you're done, give this book to a friend!

YOU HAVE TOO MANY OPTIONS!

One of the biggest challenges with Social Security—as with Medicare, the subject of my previous book, *Prepare for Medicare—The Insider's Guide* is that you have too many options. You not only have options in terms of when you start drawing your benefits, but you also have options for whether to DIY or get help from a professional.

This is both a curse and a blessing. It is a curse because the sheer amount of information can be exhausting and overwhelming. Just search "Social Security" on Google, YouTube, or Amazon, and you will never reach the end of the information and books available. Information overload is real and can make you feel that you want to put your head in the sand and avoid making a decision altogether.

But options are also an advantage because everyone's situation is different. There is no "perfect age" to start receiving Social Security benefits. It is a highly individualized decision, and there is no magic answer that will work for everyone. The solution is not to simply choose age 62 or 70. I'll go so far as to say that if anyone answers the question "When should you start drawing Social Security?" with simply an age, *run*.

So, when and what is the right decision for *you and your household*? It depends on a lot of factors, including your marital status, earnings history, age, whether or not you have children and how old they are, whether or not you have a pension, and much, much more.

Therefore, in this book, I will emphasize general strategies that apply to most people, specific strategies for various situations, and case studies that illustrate these concepts. My goal is to help you cut through the noise and narrow down the options so you can clearly see what's best for your individual situation.

WHO AM I, AND WHY DID I WRITE THIS BOOK?

As with my previous book, *Prepare for Medicare—The Insider's Guide*, I wrote *Prepare for Social Security—The Insider's Guide* to help you. I believe part of my purpose for being on Earth is to help people understand complicated things like healthcare, personal finance, and retirement issues. When it comes to Medicare and Social Security, I bring a unique and holistic perspective as an expert in both topics.

In my own life, I pursue laughter and happiness with those I love. Helping people brings me joy. I want you to be able to do the same in yours as you head toward retirement and, hopefully, many blessed years afterward. I find more meaning in my life by using my knowledge to help those who need it most.

For the last couple of decades, I have spent my professional life as a Medicare insider. I share my experience with the world through books, podcasts, television and radio appearances, YouTube videos, online courses, and partnerships. Wealth management firms, insurance companies, agents, websites, financial advisors, and tax professionals often give away "free" or very low-cost advice in hopes that you become a client of theirs or do something else that benefits them financially. There's never really a "free" lunch, is there?

They're not bad people. Some of my best friends are insurance agents and financial planners. It's just that I don't always share their perspective. I created my first book, as well as the one you're reading, to cut through the noise and share my objective advice and experience.

You can't "sell" Medicare, but Medicare insurance agents make healthy commissions selling insurance policies in and around Medicare. Helping people figure out Original Medicare Parts A and B, Medicare Advantage, Medigap, and Medicare Part D Prescription Drug Plans (PDPs) is helpful to people. But what's behind that is an entire Medicare insurance ecosystem that sells people insurance policies and financial planning products. In essence, most of the "free" Medicare education, YouTube videos, and websites out there are designed to lead you into buying an insurance policy.

Similarly, you can't "sell" Social Security, but financial planners, wealth managers, insurance agents, accountants, and annuity salespeople can certainly make commissions selling products and insurance policies around Social Security education.

Over the last 20 years, I've trained thousands of Medicare agents in live classrooms. I explained all the hoops Medicare agents have to jump through initially and annually to sell Medicare insurance products in *Prepare for Medicare—The Insider's Guide* (I'll refer you to that book for a detailed summary). Medicare certifications don't include much, if anything, about Social Security. I wondered, why not? In my experience, Medicare insurance agents and agencies are *not* usually Social Security experts, and none of the Medicare insurance companies does training on it. In addition, none of the annual certifications that agents have to take for Medicare contains much, if any, Social Security training.

All of the Medicare insurance agents I know basically understand a) you can have Medicare deduct any monthly premium you owe for Medicare Part D or a Medicare Advantage out of your Social Security check, and b) people have to decide when they're going to start getting their Social Security benefits. Yet there is a lot of interaction between Social Security and Medicare. We have an entire chapter devoted to the relationship between these two government programs, so you'll hear much more about this later.

In fact, a great Medicare agent *should* know a lot about Social Security. But they probably don't. Likewise, some financial advisors can tell you about Social Security, but they're not great at Medicare. There is a knowledge gap among lots of advisors and agents who "help" people plan for retirement. This is a gap I am excited to fill with this book.

When I decided to write this book, I *wasn't* a Social Security insider. I knew about as much as most Medicare insurance agents do, which is not enough, so I had to do a lot of research. I was an outsider. I ordered and read all the other books on Social Security and spent untold hours of research on the subject.

To top it off, I even investigated not one, but *two* professional Social Security certification programs offered to financial advisors and insurance professionals. *The National Social Security Advisor* certification has been called the "gold standard" in Social Security training and education and has been awarded to only 2,500 people across the country. I also researched the *National Association of Registered Social Security Analysts* online training program.

Between my independent research and those two certification courses meant for financial planners, wealth managers, annuity salespeople, and insurance agents, what I found was very interesting.

These programs do a good job of explaining Social Security and how to help people create strategies and personalized decisions around electing Social Security. Even beyond that, there are marketing materials and instructional "how-to's" for financial planners, agents, annuity salespeople, life insurance, lawyers, and estate planners who use Social Security as a sales lead funnel. Plus, they're pretty up-front about that. Their intentions are basically hiding in plain sight: help clients with Social Security planning and pivot them into products that generate commissions.

This is not necessarily a bad thing. For example, The Gap uses 99-cent flip-flops to lure you into the store. In business terms, it's called a "loss leader." There's no way The Gap makes any money on 99-cent flip-flops. They probably lose money when you buy the 99-cent flip-flops. But they don't care because it gets you into the store where they can sell you the jeans and shirts that *do* make them money. In the same way, lots of "experts" use Social Security information as a way to get you into their sales funnel to buy all kinds of insurance, annuities, IRA rollovers, and other products and services.

There is no shortage of financial gurus offering advice and products that you might find useful. I have an entire chapter dedicated to helping you find a competent and reputable advisor. This book will help you know what questions to ask, and understand the answers that are given.

Throughout this book, I will cite many outside sources. You can head over to https://PrepareforSocialSecurity.com/sources to view the links to those sources. I've also included a glossary of common Social Security terms and acronyms at the end of this book. Additional information and more in-depth discussion are available on the website as well. I encourage you to use the links only I provide at https://PrepareforSocialSecurity.com/sources and not click out of them, or you'll end up going down the very same rabbit hole you've no doubt already found yourself in, reading lots of random blog posts on the internet.

This is also a great time to mention the other helpful resources you'll find on my website. When you visit, you can find your local SSA office, including driving directions and phone numbers. In addition, I also offer Social Security consulting and a Prepare for Social Security course that will visually walk you through all the elements of the book, including how to determine when to file for Social Security and how to file. Don't miss these amazing resources!

MAKING THE SYSTEM WORK FOR YOU

Let's be honest: most people feel confused and frustrated by all the details that go into making a decision about when to apply for Social Security benefits.

But there is no need for it to be this hard. As we journey together through this complicated maze called Social Security, I will be your personal tour guide. I will filter out the noise and share with you only what you need to know. I don't have any interest in stuffing your head full of knowledge just to increase the page count of a book. My sole purpose is to help you feel comfortable and confident navigating Social Security so you can make wise decisions.

This book will show you how to do three things:

1. How to decide when to apply for Social Security benefits.
2. How to actually enroll.
3. How to confidently DIY (do it yourself) or find an advisor to help you navigate the maze.

Albert Einstein allegedly said, "You do not really understand something unless you can explain it to your grandmother." That's quite literally what I'm going to do: explain Social Security in clear terms that anyone can understand without having to go back to college. It's not going to be too technical, but at the same time, it's not going to be so basic and simple that you could easily find the same material online. I'll do the hard work of sorting through some pretty complex issues and cut through quickly to the bottom line you need to know.

A QUICK TOUR OF
PREPARE FOR SOCIAL SECURITY

To help you get the most out of this book, let me share a summary of each chapter so you can quickly find what you need.

CHAPTER 1: WHAT IS SOCIAL SECURITY?

This chapter will give you the big picture of Social Security. We will review what Social Security is, how and why it was created, and why you need it. We will also summarize Social Security benefits such as retirement, disability, and income for dependents and survivors. You'll learn how benefits are calculated, how credits work, and why you shouldn't believe many of the common myths that have circulated about Social Security for years.

Early in their careers, a lot of people assume that Social Security won't be there by the time they retire, or that if it is, it will pay out so little they'd be lucky to buy a loaf of bread with their monthly check. Wrong on both counts. Or, they file early because they don't want to pass away before they get back what they put in over the course of their working life.

Don't believe the hype. Social Security is one of the most firmly established programs the United States government offers. For most people, even if it is not enough by itself for all the things you'd like to do in retirement, it will provide a substantial chunk of change that you'll be grateful for to cover significant monthly expenses.

CHAPTER 2: DECIDING WHEN TO CLAIM YOUR SOCIAL SECURITY BENEFITS

This chapter gets into more specific details that are essential for you to understand. How do you enroll in Social Security? What's the best age to start drawing benefits? You'll find plenty of age-related advice out there that is overly simplistic; we have to remember that everyone's situation is different. If it's a choice between drawing Social Security versus cashing out more of your other investments to make ends meet, you might be better off retiring earlier.

But generally speaking, the best advice is to wait until age 70. Strictly from the standpoint of maximizing your money, there's no debate.

If that's the case, then why do the vast majority of people start drawing Social Security early at age 62? Many fear that if they die early, they won't get to enjoy as much of their benefits, and they maybe even know people who died without getting anything. Others falsely assume the program may run out of money before they reach 70. If you feel that way, we'll look at the evidence and see if you change your mind.

We'll also look at the most advantageous ways to manage Social Security not only for your own benefits but for those of your spouse and dependents. Unlike Medicare, with Social Security you have one-time choices to make that will impact your spouse and potentially your children.

Why should an individual or married couple take early, full, or late Social Security retirement benefits? What are the pros and cons? What are the common mistakes and misperceptions to avoid? What are some optimal strategies to consider? What if you are retiring before 65, retiring at 65, or working past 65? How should your strategy be modified if you are married or single, healthy or ill, and with or without dependents?

Many people don't realize that their spouse can receive a benefit of up to half that of the primary Social Security insurance account holder. What if your spouse passes away? You can start taking survivors benefits as early as age 60 and can receive up to 75% of your deceased spouse's benefit. It's important to bear these facts in mind so you don't leave money on the table.

CHAPTER 3: SOCIAL SECURITY ELECTION CASE STUDIES

In this chapter, we will bring it all home with case studies to illustrate different life situations. We will review the most common optimal strategies and provide case studies that can help you understand how the system works better by comparing you with someone in a similar situation. Those examples will also let you compare outcomes of drawing benefits at different ages: 62, 65, 67, or 70.

I've also put together a helpful checklist to guide you through making the best decisions related to your Social Security benefits. In addition, I'll provide you with a bibliography of good online and print sources if you want to go into more detail than we can do in a brief book, but I will get you off to a good start.

CHAPTER 4: THE "FRUSTRATING FLAWS" OF SOCIAL SECURITY

I will point out some of the frustrating flaws of Social Security that prevent it from living up to its potential. I'll also suggest ways to supplement Social Security to prevent those flaws from interfering with your post-retirement plans. Many people are unaware that Social Security benefits are taxed as income by the federal government and some state governments. This is an important consideration in making your retirement plans.

CHAPTER 5: THE SOCIAL SECURITY MARKETING MACHINE—AND WHAT IT MEANS FOR YOU

You could also call this chapter "Consumer Beware." I want to help you understand the motivations and machinery behind the marketing and "free" information related to Social Security. Many organizations, salespeople, and websites are trying to sell you access to fancy online calculators, free lunch-n-learn seminars, and other "free" information to develop a relationship.

You will often hear about the "Social Security is a fixed-rate annuity" concept. Therefore, advisors, annuity salespeople, and insurance agents could potentially guide you to maximize or hasten your benefits. This frees up money for annuities, stocks and bonds, and expensive insurance products.

CHAPTER 6: UNDERSTANDING HOW SOCIAL SECURITY AND MEDICARE WORK TOGETHER

What are the issues related to managing Medicare and Social Security together? You'll want to know that if you elect Social Security at a certain time, Medicare automatically enrolls you; otherwise, if you defer Social Security, you will need to sign up for Medicare manually.

So, what's the best strategy for how and when to sign up for Social Security and Medicare? Most people elect to have their Medicare Part D or Medicare Advantage premiums automatically deducted from their Social Security checks, which sounds convenient, until they realize that Social Security sometimes takes months to catch up to Medicare, then takes payments out all at once.

In the meantime, the Medicare insurance company may ask for a manual payment from you, leading to a double payment when Social Security finally deducts the payment. It's a mess, I know! But this is just one of the many ways things don't always work out in real life the way they are supposed to on paper, so we need to plan for them.

CHAPTER 7: FILING FOR SOCIAL SECURITY BENEFITS: DIY (DO-IT-YOURSELF)

If you want to take the DIY approach, this book will help you get started. I'll identify reputable sources of information and online calculators that will help you make wise and prudent decisions. Then I'll guide you through how to set up everything you need using the SSA.gov website, in person, or over the phone.

CHAPTER 8: FILING FOR SOCIAL SECURITY BENEFITS: HIRE A CONSULTANT/ADVISOR

For those who decide to hire a consultant or financial planner, this book will give you a basic familiarity with the ins and outs of Social Security so you can ask the right questions—and understand the answers you receive.

A whole multimillion-dollar industry has grown up just around helping people figure out Social Security. There are two types of Social Security "experts." With the first one, you'll pay a fee for a comprehensive report and custom recommendations. With the second one, you can receive advice from an "expert" who doesn't charge a consulting fee.

However, you'll find that "free" advice is not always as free as it might appear. Frankly, most people offering to help you with this issue for "free" are interested in up-selling you something else: an insurance policy, a retirement plan, a webinar, or any number of other expensive products. Unfortunately, there are also those who take advantage of the anxieties of vulnerable people for their own profit. I'll show you how to avoid those people and find the best expert for you and your family.

I'll offer you some advice on how to spot a scam and what to look for in a legitimate retirement advisor. What makes a person in this field an expert? How do you identify them? Do they have to hold any professional designations? How important is it that your advisor also be well-informed about Medicare? It all sounds overwhelming, but I'll show you how to make the most out of "free" services without getting sucked into buying anything else.

CHAPTER 9: BRINGING IT ALL TOGETHER & FORMULATING YOUR PLAN

In this chapter, we will bring everything you have learned together so you can start to develop your plan to get the most out of Social Security. We will compare and contrast the DIY and advisor/consultant approaches.

You will also learn whether to use the B/E (break-even) strategy, which is a common yet controversial approach. There are many, many factors to consider when formulating your Social Security approach, and I want you to make an informed, wise decision.

CHAPTER 10: SPECIAL SITUATIONS: VETERANS, DISABILITY, AND MORE

We'll also look at some other special situations that may apply to you and explain in plain English how you can research and understand how the rules of Social Security apply in those circumstances. For example, what are the rights of surviving spouses or divorced spouses? What about military veterans? What about clients who live abroad? We'll consider all these and more.

LET'S GET STARTED!

Before we begin Chapter 1, let me emphasize what this book is not. *Prepare for Social Security—The Insider's Guide* is not a book that takes a "curmudgeonly" or negative approach to this long-running government program. Much of the literature on Social Security talks about it like it's a burden rather than a *blessing*.

Is our current Social Security program perfect? Of course not. But it is absolutely a *benefit* in that it provides a measure of financial stability for Americans in their retirement years. That is something to celebrate! So, we will spend a lot of time in this book helping you navigate the system and taking a positive yet realistic approach.

I also want to emphasize that this book does not cover every single conceivable situation related to Social Security. We will not dive into issues and details concerning disability benefits, benefits for children, or other niche topics. This book is primarily geared toward retirees.

I started this introduction off by suggesting that the process of making decisions about Social Security is a lot like buying a computer. A lot of people feel overwhelmed by this kind of decision, want to avoid it, and honestly just wish there were someone they could trust who could help them decide what to do. You're fortunate if you have a close relative who loves technology!

Unfortunately, few of us have family members with the level of expertise in Social Security to help us out the way we need. The Social Security Administration itself is understaffed and struggling with outdated technology, so even they are not always able to give you the accurate information you need.

But knowledge is power. I want to put the knowledge—and the power—in your hands where it belongs. Knowledge accumulates as you use it. Just like you start using a computer, figuring out how things work and how to make it work for you, my hope is that I can help you become increasingly confident in your knowledge of the Social Security system so that it also will work for you. And I hope that after it's sorted out, your Social Security, like your new computer, will help you accomplish the work, family connection, and play that will make your years rich and rewarding.

One more thing: throughout this book, I'll be highlighting a few tips and observations I think are especially important. I want you to pay close attention to these, so I've indicated each one with an icon like this:

Thank you for reading. Now let's get started!

To your wealth, wisdom, and wellness!

—matt feret

Matt Feret

https://PrepareforMedicare.com

https://PrepareforSocialSecurity.com

https://PrepareforPassing.com

https://TheMattFeretShow.com

https://www.amazon.com/author/mattferet

CHAPTER ONE

WHAT IS SOCIAL SECURITY?

As you begin this book, you may be wondering whether Social Security planning is really necessary for you. Maybe you have some savings, or you're counting on your adult children or spouse to support you during retirement. Maybe you're younger and haven't thought about retirement much at all. Maybe you think the government should get out of the retirement business and let everyone take care of their own needs.

Regardless of your age, financial status, or political persuasion, there are many reasons to give Social Security planning your time and attention. Here are six of them:

1. You will likely live longer than you think. Statistically, more Americans than ever before are living into their 80s, 90s, and beyond. Every so often, we'll see a news article reporting that the average life expectancy of men and women is somewhere between 76 and 80. What they never tell you is that number is based on babies being born today!

In fact, if you're a male already past the age of 62, you're statistically very likely to live until you're nearly 85 years old! Females who reach age 62 are very likely to live to age 87! This is according to the very same people responsible for paying Social Security benefits: the Social Security Administration! (Source: https://PrepareforSocialSecurity.com/sources.)

One of the real advantages of being a citizen of the U.S. is enjoying access to a high standard of living, abundant nutritional options, and groundbreaking medical science. However, outside the U.S., very few other "wealthy" nations require their retirees to make high-stakes, complex financial decisions later in life. Therefore, much of the responsibility of making wise retirement decisions and supporting yourself in retirement is on you, the individual. What will you live on if your private savings and investments give out by the time you're 70? You can fall back on Social Security, which pays benefits every month for the rest of your life.

2. You might not work as long as you think. Although people are living longer on average than in decades past, disability and death unfortunately happen quite early in life for some people. Even if you stay perfectly healthy, it's also possible that you will lose your job as the economy changes and you get older.

How easy would it be at 62 years old to find a new job that could support yourself and your family? Social Security can give you the margin to be able to work one or more part-time jobs rather than needing to land another high-paying career. (Yes, believe it or not, once you reach full retirement age, you can work and still receive Social Security benefits without penalty.)

3. You have people counting on you. You might be a younger worker providing for a stay-at-home spouse and dependent children. Who will care for them if you become disabled or pass away at an early age? Multigenerational families are becoming increasingly common, with older adults helping to support their adult children or raise their grandchildren using income from Social Security. Women tend to have longer lifespans and lower lifetime earnings than men. Widows may easily fall into poverty without the survivors benefits of Social Security.

4. Many people do not have access to employer-sponsored 401(k) plans or employer pensions. Just over half of U.S. workers have access to 401(k) plans sponsored by their employers, and even then, not everyone chooses to participate. In addition, fewer companies are offering pensions as an employee benefit. Many companies opt to hire part-time workers, and more people than ever are participating in the "gig economy" by working multiple short-term contract jobs with no retirement provisions. Many retirees will simply not have any option other than Social Security once they retire or become disabled (source: https://PrepareforSocialSecurity.com/sources).

5. Social Security is a stable, substantial source of income. There are always inherent risks to investing in stocks, bonds, real estate, or unconventional instruments such as cryptocurrencies. An ill-timed market fluctuation could erase years of growth from your nest egg just when you need it most. By contrast, Social Security benefits continue for a lifetime and are adjusted for inflation so that rising costs don't erode your living standard in retirement.

The benefits can be substantial. A 66-year-old retiree who receives the current maximum monthly benefit of $3,345 will receive more than $400,000 if they live only ten years, $890,000 if they live 20 years, and $1.5 million over 30 years (assuming an annual cost of living adjustment of 2.8%).

6. Social Security supplements your retirement plan. For most older Americans, Social Security provides the lion's share of their income. For about 27% of seniors, Social Security provides 90% or more of their income. So, chances are high that Social Security will make up a large chunk, if not the majority, of your income as a retiree (source: https://PrepareforSocialSecurity.com/sources).

If you have been farsighted and fortunate enough to save up a nest egg, Social Security benefits can cover some of your expenses so that you don't have to dip into high-return investments earlier than you want to. If your investments are not sufficient for all your retirement needs, Social Security will at least reduce the amount you will have to find through part-time work, help from family members, or other means to keep you reasonably supported in your latter years.

For many people, retirement planning can be understandably anxiety-provoking. We might feel like it's all we can do to make ends meet in our current circumstances, much less worrying about how we will manage in the future with potentially poorer health, less income, and fewer prospects to pull ourselves up by the bootstraps. Yet despite recent economic uncertainties, many Americans are optimistic about their retirement. You can be, too.

A January 2021 survey by the Employee Benefit Research Institute found that confidence in Social Security had reached an all-time high—72% of retirees and 53% of workers said they were somewhat or very confident that Social Security would continue to pay the same benefits in the future. Eighty percent of retirees expressed confidence that they would live comfortably throughout their retirement (source: https://PrepareforSocialSecurity.com/sources).

One of the contributing factors to this optimism was that Social Security continued making payments on schedule through an intense national crisis. This stressful period included sharp market fluctuations, hundreds of thousands of deaths from the pandemic, the loss of millions of jobs, and a major economic restructuring. As a result, a significant portion of working people made career changes or decided to work from home permanently.

Of course, public sentiment can be fickle and inaccurate, but actual economic behavior backs up this optimism. Furthermore, long-term data on the spending habits of retirees show that their living expenses tend to decrease, especially as they pay off their mortgages and relocate to smaller homes with lower taxes. Such situations promise to help older adults stretch their retirement dollars even further.

The Social Security system itself also has some genuine strengths that give us legitimate reasons for optimism:

- It is backed by the United States government and powerful political interests.
- It reliably pays monthly benefits to qualified retirees and the disabled.
- It gives you the flexibility to decide when to retire so that you can adjust your benefits to your family situation.
- It supports low-income workers based on years of work rather than their income level.
- It provides non-working married people with a benefit of 50% of their working spouse's benefit. This benefit is also available to divorced spouses.

- ✓ It allows you to continue working during retirement to supplement your income if you choose.
- ✓ It provides for you, your spouse, and your dependents in the event of your death or disability.
- ✓ It provides inflation-adjusted monthly payments, guaranteed for life.

Even if you're convinced Social Security can benefit you in retirement and you feel optimistic that it will continue to support you and your survivors, it can still be intimidating to navigate the bureaucracy of the program. Over the past several years, Congress has cut the operating budget for the Social Security Administration by 13% even as the number of Social Security recipients increased by 21%. As a result, the SSA has had to close field offices and reduce staff, which has increased wait times and reduced the quality of customer service (source: https://PrepareforSocialSecurity.com/sources).

Those who are comfortable with computer technology can try to research the answers to their questions on the SSA website (ssa.gov). However, it contains a vast amount of information that can be difficult to navigate and understand for people who are not comfortable with technology or have certain disabilities.

That said, if you are intentional about your Social Security choices and plan correctly with the help of responsible financial advisors and books like this one, you don't need to be intimidated by the bureaucracy. Millions of people have navigated this system before you, and millions more will after you. You can do it, too.

A BRIEF HISTORY OF SOCIAL SECURITY

Self-sufficiency is one of the hallmarks of American culture. In generations past, families took care of each other and didn't expect the government to step in to help them through hard times.

During the Great Depression, though, the country faced a crisis unlike any in its history. Unemployment reached 25%, people's life savings were wiped out, and half of the senior population found themselves living in poverty. People who left their family farms to seek work in the cities didn't have access to their loved ones and community support networks.

Meanwhile, European countries had begun to experiment with social insurance—the idea of using insurance methods to protect the population from economic downturns to benefit all of society. The idea had many detractors in the United States who considered it a dangerous step toward socialism. Others felt it was essential to protect vulnerable Americans and save the country from potential social unrest. Following much debate, Congress finally passed the Social Security Act, which was signed into law by Franklin D. Roosevelt in 1935.

In its original form, Social Security tried to mitigate the effects of old age, disabilities, poverty, unemployment, and the struggles of surviving spouses and dependent children. In the first 20 years of the program, debates focused on expanding it to include more occupational groups to make sure the program was properly funded.

Beginning in the early 1950s, the program was expanded to provide more benefits. The government tried to strike a balance between promoting equality while at the same time providing the necessary protection for low-income workers.

Social Security was conceived as a self-financing program with contributions from employers and employees, with no money contributed by the U.S. Treasury to fund its benefits. It was not to be a social welfare program that would discourage people from working. Instead, it was envisioned as a social insurance program that would partially replace earnings lost to retirement, disability, or death for workers and their families.

The core of the program has continued to survive, with some changes:

- In 1950, husbands and widowers became eligible for benefits.
- By 1955, it had been expanded to cover more people, including farmers, the self-employed, the military, and government workers.

- ✓ Disability benefits were added in 1956.

- ✓ An option for early retirement at age 62 was added in 1956 for women and in 1961 for men.

- ✓ Medicare was added in 1965 to provide health insurance.

- ✓ Benefit payments and Social Security taxes have increased over time.

Today only 76% of those who receive Social Security are retired workers. The remainder are survivors, children, or disabled workers. More than $1 trillion of the program's funding comes through payroll taxes. Employers and employees each pay 6.2% of earnings, and those who are self-employed pay the full 12.4% themselves. A further $108 billion of the program's funding comes from interest earnings and taxation of Social Security benefits (source: https://PrepareforSocialSecurity.com/sources).

Social Security ran a surplus every year from 1982 to 2020 but began running a deficit in 2021. This was due not only to the financial shock of the pandemic but also to the long-term demographic challenge of an aging population. The Baby Boomers are a very large cohort of the population who had relatively few children. Combined with lengthened lifespans, this means the American population overall is aging rapidly. In 1945, there were 41.9 workers paying into the program for each retiree receiving benefits; today, that number is only 2.8 workers per retiree (source: https://PrepareforSocialSecurity.com/sources).

The 2023 Social Security Trustees report estimated that Social Security can continue paying full benefits only until 2033. If Congress does not act to solve funding issues, benefits will have to be reduced after that date (source: https://PrepareforSocialSecurity.com/sources).

Reforms such as tax increases, benefit reductions, alternative investment plans, or growing the taxpaying workforce through immigration are some possible ways to close the funding gap and avoid cutting benefits. Due to the political sensitivity of these issues, Congress is unlikely to take action on them until it becomes unavoidable.

Most analysts agree, though, that people currently receiving benefits or nearing the point of retirement will be included on the existing benefit levels and will not have to worry about a major reduction in their benefits.

DISPELLING COMMON MYTHS ABOUT SOCIAL SECURITY

Given the complexity of the Social Security program and how it has changed over the years, it's not surprising that there is a lot of misinformation floating around about it. If you act upon inaccurate information, you might receive less than you're owed from Social Security each month. Therefore, it's important to know facts from myths.

Here are 14 myths that need to be laid to rest:

Myth 1: You should claim your benefits early to make sure you get your "fair share."

Fact: If you do not reach your full life expectancy (due to health problems, for example), waiting to claim your benefits will reduce the overall amount you receive during your retirement. If you reach or exceed your life expectancy, then waiting until you are 70 to maximize your monthly benefits would be a wiser course of action.

Myth 2: You will never get back all you have paid into Social Security.

Fact: Those who live a long time may receive more than they contributed to the program. It provides a guaranteed lifetime income during retirement for you, and continues to provide for your surviving spouse for the rest of their life after you pass away.

Myth 3: Stocks are a better investment.

Fact: Stock investments take time to accumulate. If you become disabled or pass away at an early age, your nest egg may not be large enough to provide sufficiently for you, your dependent family members, and your survivors. If stocks decline suddenly in your later years, there may not be enough time to rebuild your savings before you need them.

Myth 4: Your Social Security benefits always go up each year due to cost-of-living increases.

Fact: The cost-of-living adjustment is connected to the prices of an index of consumer goods. When prices of goods on this index show an increase, then benefits are increased. But in years of low inflation, such as 2010, 2011, and 2016, there was no cost-of-living increase.

Myth 5: Social Security benefits are tax-free.

Fact: Starting in 1984, a portion of Social Security benefits became federally taxable based on your income level. For single people, benefits become taxable when your combined income exceeds $25,000. For married couples filing jointly, the threshold is $32,000. (Combined income is the total of your adjusted gross income, non-taxable interest earnings, and half of your Social Security benefit.) Social Security benefits are also subject to taxes at the state level in some states. See the link in the Appendix to check your state's tax policy.

Myth 6: If you keep working, you can lose your benefits permanently.

Fact: People who claim benefits before full retirement age and keep working may have a portion of their benefits withheld, depending on whether their income exceeds an earnings limit and how close they are to full retirement age. You will get that money back, but not in one lump sum. Instead, Social Security will increase your benefit when you reach full retirement age to account for the money they previously withheld. Once you reach full retirement age, there is no benefit reduction, no matter your income level.

Myth 7: Your benefits will be negatively affected if you divorce your spouse.

Fact: If you were married for ten years consecutively, have not remarried, and have reached your full retirement age, you may receive either your own benefit or 50% of your ex-spouse's benefit, whichever is higher. You do not have to talk to your ex-spouse about this. It does not matter how long you have been divorced. It will not hurt their benefit for you to place a claim based on their income level, and you should do so if it results in a higher monthly payment for you than a claim based on your own income.

Myth 8: You can claim benefits at 62, then increase them when you reach full retirement age of 66-67 or more.

Fact: Once you have claimed your Social Security retirement benefit, you cannot increase it. However, you can "suspend" your benefit after you reach full retirement age and resume it by age 70. If you do so, your benefit will increase by 8% for each year of delay. Subsequently, you will receive a cost of living increase each year, but there will be no increase in your base benefit. And this benefit will start automatically when you reach age 70 unless you indicate differently to the Social Security Administration.

It is important to note that you can no longer use the "file and suspend" strategy that allowed you to file and then suspend your benefits while your spouse continued to collect a benefit. Some couples used this strategy to have their cake and eat it, too—essentially increasing one person's eventual earnings by filing and then delaying, while at the same time collecting a spousal benefit.

You could only use this strategy if you reached your full retirement age before April 30, 2016 and then suspended your benefits. Congress changed the rules in November 2015. You can still file for Social Security and then suspend your benefits, but your spouse will not be able to collect a spousal benefit while your own benefits are suspended.

Myth 9: Retired military personnel cannot receive both their military pension and Social Security.

Fact: The Social Security Administration does not reduce benefits because of military retirement benefits. This means active-duty service members may receive both their military pension and Social Security benefits. And since 1988, even those on inactive military duty (such as weekend drills) have also been covered by Social Security.

Myth 10: The Social Security system has contributed to our huge national debt.

Fact: For almost every one of the past 40 years, Social Security has generated a surplus, reducing the overall United States national debt.

Myth 11: Members of Congress don't pay into the system.

Fact: Since 1984, members of Congress, the President, the Vice President, federal judges, and most political appointees are required to pay Social Security taxes and follow the same rules as ordinary citizens.

Myth 12: Undocumented immigrants receive benefits illegally.

Fact: Some undocumented immigrants submit false Social Security numbers to get jobs. They pay taxes into the system but usually don't try to collect benefits, so they actually improve the program's bottom line by an estimated $13 billion a year (source: https://PrepareforSocialSecurity.com/sources).

Myth 13: Seniors are wealthy and do not need Social Security.

Fact: More than half of retirees depend on Social Security for 50% or more of their income in retirement. Without Social Security, an estimated 37.8% of Americans age 65 and older would live below the poverty line. With Social Security, only 9% of this age group lives below poverty. Furthermore, a growing number of retirees support their adult children and grandchildren (source: https://PrepareforSocialSecurity.com/sources).

Myth 14: The government raids Social Security for other programs.

Fact: Social Security is separate from the federal government's general fund. By law, Social Security funds are invested in special U.S. Treasury bonds that must be repaid with interest. The government has always repaid these in full. The revenue from interest payments adds approximately $76 billion to the program annually.

As you can see, these myths are far from the mark and can adversely affect the amount of your Social Security benefits. In addition, they can cause you to be frustrated by problems that do not exist. This is not to say the program is without any problems, but simply that there are enough *real* problems to work through that we do not need to be distracted by rumors not based on facts.

Now let's take a brief look at what you actually get when you start receiving Social Security benefits.

A SUMMARY OF SOCIAL SECURITY BENEFITS

We all know that Social Security provides retirement benefits, but fewer people realize that it also covers disability and provides benefits for survivors after they die. These benefits can be especially crucial for younger families that experience the tragic loss of the family's primary wage earner.

Benefits are allocated based on "credits." Currently, you receive one credit for approximately $1,500 you earn that is subject to Social Security tax, with a maximum of four per year. The earnings figure for Social Security credits changes each year to keep pace with wages in the country. You can review your earnings record by visiting the Social Security Administration website.

To receive retirement benefits, workers born after 1929 need 40 credits to receive full benefits (or be "fully insured") by Social Security. In most cases, this requires that you work for at least ten years. In some cases, a person without enough work credits may be able to work part-time until they earn enough credits to be eligible.

It is also possible to qualify for retirement benefits based on a spouse's work history. Retirement benefits may be claimed as early as age 62 and as late as age 70, with higher monthly benefits paid for life if a later retirement date is chosen. This is a great strategy if you are in good health and do not need your retirement benefits earlier because you're still working or have other investment income you prefer to draw upon.

Although this book does not go in depth on the Social Security Disability Insurance (SSDI) and Supplemental Security Income (SSI) programs, I want to mention them briefly here. These programs provide assistance to adults and children who have disabilities and little income or other financial resources. The amount of the benefit depends on your age at the time you become disabled.

Before age 24, you can receive benefits if you earned six credits in the three years before your disability started. From 24-31, you need credits for at least half the time between age 21 and the year of your disability. From 31-42, you need at least 20 credits. Starting at age 43, you need 20 credits plus one extra credit for each year you are older than 42. (For example, at 43 you need 21 credits, while at 44, you need 22 credits.) If the disability happens at age 62 or older, you need 40 credits to draw disability. If you qualify for these programs, you would probably be best served by engaging a law firm specializing in disability benefits.

Social Security survivors benefits are paid to widows, widowers, and dependents of eligible workers. Survivors benefits do not always require you to have earned a full 40 credits. If you die, your surviving spouse may receive benefits if you have worked at least 1.5 years of the 3.25 years prior to your death. When someone passes away, the Social Security Administration should be notified as soon as possible. In most cases, funeral homes will do so for the deceased if you provide them with their Social Security number. Alternatively, you can phone the SSA to report a death, but you cannot do so through the website.

Social Security benefits are available for your dependents if they have a parent who is disabled or retired and entitled to Social Security benefits, or if they have a parent who has died after working long enough to be eligible for benefits. In some cases, benefits are also available to stepchildren, grandchildren, step-grandchildren, or adopted children. Eligible dependents must be unmarried and meet one of the following criteria:

- Be younger than 18
- Be between 18 and 19 and a full-time high school student
- Be 18 or older with a disability that began before age 22

The intention of benefits for dependents is to stabilize family finances and make it possible for minors to complete high school. Children can receive up to 50% of their parent's retirement or disability benefits. In the case of a parent's death, children can get up to 75% of the parent's Social Security benefit. However, there is a ceiling to the amount Social Security will pay to a family, which totals 150% to 180% of the parent's full benefit amount. If the amount paid to all family members together goes over this limit, each child's benefit is reduced proportionately to get the family total down to the maximum allowed amount.

HOW TO SIGN UP FOR SOCIAL SECURITY

To receive Social Security retirement benefits, you can claim as early as age 62 or as late as 70. Spousal and survivors benefits can be claimed at other ages, but the first big decision you need to make is when you want your benefits to start. For each year you wait, up to age 70, your monthly benefits will be higher for the rest of your life. This is a great choice for someone who has every reason to anticipate living to their full life expectancy or beyond.

It is important to note that you don't *have* to start collecting Social Security by age 70. No one is going to force you to start drawing benefits, nor will they automatically start. But if you wait past age 70, the benefits of waiting past your full retirement age stop adding up.

Those with disabilities or chronic health issues who have reason to think they may not reach full life expectancy may be better advised to begin drawing benefits earlier. There is no "one size fits all" answer to this question. Rather, it depends on careful consideration of your individual circumstances.

You can file your application up to four months before the date you want your benefits to start. It's best to apply as soon as possible within this time frame since it can take six weeks to process an application, and the Social Security Administration may contact you for additional information, documents, or clarification. It takes 30-60 days after the application is approved for you to receive your first payment. If you file your application late, you can receive up to six months of missed benefits as a lump sum. If you wait any longer than six months, those extra months of payments will be lost (source: https://PrepareforSocialSecurity.com/sources).

(It's helpful to note that the lump sum option potentially lowers your overall monthly benefit and, therefore, the total amount you receive over your lifetime, since it basically back-dates the application.)

There are four ways to file for Social Security benefits:

1. Complete a paper application, then mail it in or deliver it in person to a Social Security Administration office.
2. Complete an application with the help of a Social Security Administration employee in an SSA office. Make an appointment to avoid a long wait time.
3. Phone the SSA at 800-772-1213 to complete the application over the phone with a representative. Depending on the time you call, wait times may be substantial.
4. Open a "*my Social Security*" account on the SSA website and complete an online application.

Regardless of the method you choose, be aware that due to the complexities of the Social Security Program, inadequate training, and a high work volume, some SSA representatives may not know all the rules relevant to you. They may also try to talk you into choosing an option that is not best for your situation. It's important that you enlist the help of an advisor or do your own research.

If you or the Social Security Administration makes a mistake in the application process, you can appeal to the SSA to change their decision. Once you receive a letter from the SSA with their decision on your application, you must make any appeals within 60 days, in writing. You can pursue your appeal up through four levels to try to get the results you want:

1. A reconsideration by a different representative than the one who oversaw your application.
2. A hearing before an administrative law judge.
3. A review by the Social Security Administration's Appeals Council.
4. A review by the federal courts.

Each level of appeal has a 60-day filing period plus five additional days for mail delivery. In addition to this formal appeals process, you can also hire a legal firm to help or reach out to your U.S. congressional representative for assistance in expediting the process.

You also have the option of withdrawing your application entirely and starting again within the first 12 months of receiving benefits. However, the downside is that you will be required to repay all benefits received up to that point. In addition, the reapplication process will delay the start date of your newly calculated benefits.

In discussions about when to file for Social Security, the question inevitably comes up, "What happens if I don't file? Will I automatically start getting benefits?" The short answer is that the SSA is not going to start sending you money without you asking for it. **Nobody is going to force you to file for Social Security at any point. Just keep in mind that your benefits will not increase if you wait past age 70 to file. In general, the longer you wait to file, the greater your benefits will be, but this advantage ceases once you turn 70 because the retirement credits stop accruing then.**

However, there is one scenario in which your benefits will automatically begin at age 70. If you applied after you reached your full retirement age, then suspended your benefits until age 70, those benefits will automatically restart when you turn 70.

HOW SOCIAL SECURITY BENEFITS ARE CALCULATED

The Social Security Administration will calculate your benefits for you, but they do make mistakes. You should have a general awareness of how benefits are calculated so that, even if you do not feel confident in calculating them yourself, you will be better prepared to hear the explanations of Social Security personnel when you ask questions about your benefits. If you want to dive into these details, here is how to go about calculating your benefits.

The first step is to adjust your income for inflation. (You can find the inflation calculator from the Bureau of Labor Statistics by visiting https://PrepareforSocialSecurity.com/links.) When you do this, your benefit amount will better reflect the actual cost of living. This means for each year you worked through age 59, the Social Security Administration will multiply your income by a percentage for inflation, increasing your recorded earnings. For example, if you earned $10,000 in 1980, this would be multiplied by 4.1671768, and your income would be recorded as $41,671 for that year. Any earnings after age 60 are not adjusted for inflation.

The second step in figuring your benefits is to determine your Average Indexed Monthly Earnings (AIME). The Social Security Administration will pick out the highest 35 years of income you earned, substituting zeros for any years short of 35 you worked. They divide the total of these years by 420 (the number of months in 35 years) to determine your average monthly income, adjusted for inflation. **Obviously, it's important to make sure every year of your income is correctly reported to the SSA, as even one incorrect or missing year will reduce your lifetime benefits.**

Finally, your Primary Insurance Amount (PIA)—your benefit at full retirement age—is calculated. This can be a little tricky because Social Security is set up to provide more income for those who need the financial support most. To achieve this, each year, the Social Security Administration provides three so-called "bend points" that adjust benefits depending on AIME levels. Income in the first band of income is multiplied by 90%. Additional income beyond band one is multiplied by 32% at the second band level. Income that exceeds the maximum parameter of band two is multiplied by 15%.

The exact income levels for each band, or bend point, change each year, so be sure to use the one for the year you turn 62 if you want to estimate your benefit amount. The lower your average lifetime earnings, the higher the percentage of those earnings you will receive in benefits.

To give you a ballpark example of what this could look like: if you have earned under $30,000 a year, your benefit might add up to about 50% of your earnings. However, those earning near the maximum in the years before retirement may receive a benefit of about 20% of their earnings.

The age you choose to retire has a great impact on the amount of your benefits. Although you can retire as early as age 62, the Social Security Administration has established a "full retirement age" based on your date of birth, ranging from 65 for those born in 1937 and earlier to 67 for those born in 1960 or later. Retiring early for your age can reduce your monthly benefits by up to 30%, while waiting until the maximum age of 70 will give you the maximum monthly benefit, for life.

NORMAL RETIREMENT AGE

YEAR OF BIRTH	AGE
1937 and prior	65
1938	65 and 2 months
1939	65 and 4 months
1940	65 and 6 months
1941	65 and 8 months
1942	65 and 10 months
1943-54	66
1955	66 and 2 months
1956	66 and 4 months
1957	66 and 6 months
1958	66 and 8 months
1959	66 and 10 months
1960 and later	67

NOTES:
1. Persons born on January 1 of any year should refer to the normal retirement age for the previous year.
2. For the purpose of determining benefit reductions for the early retirement age, widows and widowers whose entitlement is based on having attained age 60 should add 2 years to the year of birth shown in the table.

It is possible to work while drawing Social Security or survivors benefits, and doing so could even raise, rather than decrease, the amount of your benefits. This is because the SSA reviews wages reported by Social Security recipients every year. If your earnings the previous year were one of your all-time highest-earning years, your benefit will be recalculated and increased, starting with January of the year after you earned the money.

However, your benefit may be reduced if you earn more than the annual earnings limit set by the SSA. You can consult the "Maximum Taxable Earnings" chart for the current year's earnings limit (source: https://PrepareforSocialSecurity.com/sources).

If you have not yet reached full retirement age and exceed the yearly earnings limit, your benefits may be reduced at a rate of $1 from your benefit payments for every $2 you earn above the annual limit. The year you reach your full retirement age, $1 is deducted for every $3 you earn above a different limit, which is currently more than $50,000. Further, at full retirement age, no matter how much you earn, your earnings will no longer reduce your benefits.

Income that is considered for a possible reduction of benefits includes wages, bonuses, or commissions from a job, vacation pay, or net profits if you are self-employed. Income that is *not* counted against the earnings limit includes pensions, annuities, investment income, interest, veteran's benefits, or other government or military retirement benefits.

Given all these variables, what is the bottom line? The challenge is that there are so many variables to consider that it's hard to give a one-size-fits-all answer to whether you should continue working or not. You will find some helpful advice from the SSA if you are interested in learning more. Visit https://PrepareforSocialSecurity.com/links and look for "Receiving Benefits While Working."

A FEW THOUGHTS ABOUT THE FUTURE OF SOCIAL SECURITY

Media reports, rumors, and conspiracy theories about Social Security can be frightening because of the vulnerability we all feel around aging and end-of-life issues. Some of these falsehoods are so ridiculous they can be quickly dismissed. However, other questions about the future of Social Security have some basis in fact and should be seriously considered.

Probably the most significant objection to Social Security is that it is going to run out. Many younger workers assume Social Security won't be there for them when they need it, or that the benefits will be too small to do them much good. Many older people choose to claim their full retirement benefits at the earliest possible age because they fear the program will run out of money before they are able to withdraw the full benefits they have earned.

This fear is understandable, as politicians for the past several decades have alerted the public to the fact that in its current form, Social Security will be unable to pay full benefits past the year 2033. In 2021, the program ran its first deficit since the 1980s and is expected to begin doing so on a regular basis as the number of retirees increases and the number of workers to pay into the system declines.

But even as the Social Security trust fund spends down its funds, the program will continue to have a steady revenue stream through payroll taxes that will ensure it will continue to exist in some form into the indefinite future. Many analysts predict that regardless of their current age, most workers can expect to receive at least 75% of currently promised benefits. Those who are most likely to see reduced benefits are people with higher incomes ($250,000 or more) and younger workers. Those who are closer to retirement at the time any decreases in benefits are made—say within ten years—are likely to be included into the current program and will not see a benefit decrease at all.

It is impossible to foresee how unexpected future events such as pandemics, recessions, and international conflicts may impact Social Security. Because it is such a hot-button political issue, we can easily imagine that Congress will delay taking action to reform the system until it becomes an unavoidable necessity to do so.

Indeed, Social Security has often been referred to as a "third rail" in American politics that will electrocute anyone who tries to touch it! However, it *has* been reformed many times since its inception, and we can expect it will be reformed again in the future as necessary, even if the process of doing so is politically messy.

What's the bottom line? Despite its faults and its detractors, Social Security has been successful in mitigating poverty among older adults, the disabled, and their dependents. It continues to be a significant revenue stream for most Americans in their later years, even for those who have been able to accumulate their own savings privately or through employer pension plans. The program has a long-term stable funding base in the form of payroll taxes paid by employers and employees. It is ultimately backed by the United States government itself. It is difficult to see how the program could be allowed to collapse unless the government itself ceased functioning.

Those are big-picture issues, but what does this all mean for you as an individual? The most important thing to keep in mind is that Social Security is not some kind of government handout. It is a benefit that you have earned over a lifetime of work. Your benefits are *your* hard-earned money. The stakes for you and your dependents are high enough that it is worth your while to take the time to understand as well as possible how the system works and how to maximize the benefits you receive from it.

With that in mind, read on with the determination to make this program work for you!

CHAPTER TWO

DECIDING WHEN TO FILE FOR SOCIAL SECURITY

As you near retirement age, perhaps the single most important decision you will make about Social Security is when to claim your benefits. There is no "one size fits all" answer to this question. Some people will profit most by retiring as early as possible. Others would come out better financially in the end by waiting.

If you're married, you and your spouse might want to retire at different ages to maximize your family income during retirement. You have to decide what is best for you based on a number of different factors, not all of which are purely financial. No worries. I'll take you through the process, and by the end of this chapter, you should have a clearer idea of when you want to claim your benefits and why that is the right choice for you.

WHAT DETERMINES YOUR BENEFIT AMOUNT?

How big can you expect your monthly Social Security check to be? Your benefits are calculated based on the average of your 35 highest-earning years of work, and different formulas are applied depending on the year you were born. Those with lower lifetime earnings will receive a higher percentage of their earnings in benefits.

What if you have less than 35 years of earnings? The Social Security Administration enters a "0" for each year without earnings, which reduces your monthly retirement benefit amount. Think back to middle school math class. If you failed to turn in an assignment and got a "0" score, what happened to your overall grade? The same principle applies here: **if at all possible, you need to keep working until you have no zeros in any of the 35 years of your work record.**

What if you choose to work for more than 35 years? This can actually be a great strategy if you are still in good health, have a job you like (or start a new career), and have some low-earning years on your work record you'd like to replace. If any of the years you work past your existing 35-year work record are at a higher income level, your lower-earning years will be automatically replaced with your higher-earning years. This will increase your overall benefit amount when you do start drawing Social Security.

WHEN TO CLAIM YOUR BENEFITS

Social Security rules allow you to start receiving benefits as early as age 62 or as late as age 70. The longer you wait, the higher your monthly benefit check will be.

As we discussed in Chapter 1, you should *not* be concerned that Social Security will "run out" if you don't claim your benefits early. However, you *should* be concerned about the far more possible scenario that making an ill-informed choice could cause you to leave money on the table. Drawing Social Security too early is the number one mistake retirees make in this process.

So how do you decide when to claim benefits? A key consideration is your "full retirement age" (FRA). This number is not the same for everyone since it depends on the year you were born. To give one example, retirees born in 1960 or later have an FRA of 67. People who claim their benefits before this age will lose as much as 30% of what they would have received had they waited until their FRA. This reduction is permanent, and the money is lost forever.

What if, on the other hand, you keep working past your FRA? You'll get a delayed retirement credit of 8% for each additional year you wait until age 70. So someone born in 1960 would get 124% of their full retirement benefit if they waited until 70 to start Social Security. And you would draw this higher monthly benefit for the rest of your life (source: https://PrepareforSocialSecurity.com/sources).

Some argue that it's better to take retirement early because that will give you more benefit checks over your lifetime than if you wait. **It doesn't matter how many checks you get, though—what matters is the total those checks add up to.** Taking early benefits makes each check smaller than it otherwise would have been. Waiting until age 70 results in fewer checks but a much higher monthly benefit. In the end, people who live a full lifespan will get the greatest benefit from waiting until the maximum allowable age.

One approach to determining when you should retire is your "break-even" age. This is the age when the dollar value of claiming benefits later equals the value of taking them early. It's hard to calculate this number exactly because of annual cost-of-living increases and income changes for people who are still working. However, it's possible to get a ballpark idea using a benefits calculator such as the one found on your Social Security account.

Is it more important for you to start receiving Social Security checks earlier in your retirement, giving you more checks during your lifetime (but with smaller amounts in each check)? Or would you rather wait to file later, giving you larger monthly checks but fewer overall checks in retirement?

The answer to that question is a big clue to helping you determine when to file. **If you die before you reach your break-even age, it would be better to start collecting benefits earlier. If you live beyond your break-even age, you will come out ahead in the long run.** Nobody can predict the future, of course, but it's helpful to take into account your family health history, your current health, and how long the people in your family live on average.

To help illustrate the concept of the "break-even" age, let's consider the following scenario.

COMPARISON OF BENEFITS			
	JAMES	TRACY	JACKIE
Retirement age	62	67	70
Monthly benefit	$700	$1,000	$1,240
SS income after 1 year	$8,400	$12,000	$14,880
SS income after 5 years	$42,000	$60,000	$74,400
Break-even age	n/a	11 years and 8 months	10 years and 4 months

Let's imagine two co-workers, James and Tracy, who were both born in 1960. Their full retirement age is 67. Let's imagine that if they waited until their FRA to retire, they would each begin receiving $1,000 a month.

James decides to retire in 2022 at age 62. As a result, his benefits are reduced by 30%, giving him a monthly Social Security check of $700. In his first year of retirement, he brings in $8,400. By the time five years have passed, and he reaches FRA, he has already brought in $42,000, and Tracy has received *nothing!* Sorry, Tracy.

But… when Tracy retires in 2027 at age 67, she begins drawing $1,000 a month. She's getting $300 a month more than James now, which adds up to $3,600 more than him by the end of the year. How many years of this will it take her to catch up to him and his $42,000 head start? Divide $42,000 by $3,600 and you get 11 years and eight months. So then, at age 78 and eight months, the total benefits James and Tracy have received would be equal: this is their break-even age. After this point, Tracy will continue to pull ahead. If they both live another ten years, she will be $36,000 ahead of James.

Is there anything we overlooked? Oh yes, we forgot about Jackie over there in the next cubicle. She was also born in 1960. She decides to work past FRA and wait until age 70, the maximum, to retire. When she does, her benefits are 124% of what they would have been at FRA, giving her a benefit of $1,240 a month.

James, by this point, is $67,200 ahead of her; Tracy retired just three years earlier and is only $10,800 ahead of her. But Jackie makes $540 a month ($6,480 a year) more than James. It takes her about ten years and four months to break even with him. But she makes $240 a month ($2,880 a year) more than Tracy. It takes her three years and nine months to break even with her.

Let's say she goes on to live to be 88. After these break-even points, in her remaining retirement years, she will receive about $49,442 more than James (88 - 80.37 = 7.63 years x $6,480) and about $41,040 more than Tracy (88-73.75 = 14.25 years x $2,880).

Before we jump to the conclusion that Jackie and Tracy made better choices than James, consider this: Tracy needs to live to at least 78 and eight months to break even with James, and only then does her choice to wait until FRA make sense. Jackie would have to live to be 80 and four months to break even with him. If either of them passed away sooner than that, James would actually have come out ahead of them.

Of course, it's not a competition. Let's just think about James himself. If he is in great health, has other pension plans or a job he enjoys, and knows the men in his family tend to live a long time, then it might make sense to wait to claim benefits at FRA or beyond. If he has no other means of support, has extended unemployment, needs to care for dependents, or has a serious illness or accident that shortens his lifespan, then the choice to draw benefits early might make sense.

Generally speaking, if you think you will live past your break-even age, it might be best to wait until your FRA or longer. If you have reason to think you might not live that long, then it might be better to start benefits early.

Be aware that many Social Security experts tell people not to use the break-even strategy. It can cost you a lot of money if you end up living longer than expected (although it's a great thing to live longer than expected!). Deciding the best age to retire is not a precise science. You

should consider your health and other financial resources before making a decision.

If you are more concerned about how much your total benefits will be over your whole life, then the break-even approach may appeal to you. If you care more about getting the highest monthly benefit possible, then you may decide that delaying filing for Social Security is the right choice for you.

Let's be honest. None of us wants to think about life expectancy. Inside each of us still lives that 18-year-old just starting out in life with big dreams and plans. Yet somehow, we blinked, and 50 years passed. What we look like outside might not match how we feel—and who we are—inside.

Soul-searching existential advice is beyond the scope of this book, but I remind myself that people die at all ages every day—some very young—some extraordinarily old. What I can do is be grateful for the gift of each day and fill it with as much life as possible. And if I think I might have less time left than I'd like, then that is all the more reason to live each day doing the things I love, with the people I love. Isn't that what retirement decisions are all about? We do some uncomfortable thinking now so that we can have a more comfortable experience for the many years to come.

With that in mind, let's talk quickly about life expectancy. The Social Security Administration provides a convenient Life Actuarial Table, which you can access via https://PrepareforSocialSecurity.com/links. Alternatively, they also provide a Life Expectancy Calculator, which you can access via the Links page as well. When you enter your sex and date of birth, the system will generate a chart indicating the average number of additional years you can expect to live, on average, after reaching a specific age.

According to the chart, a 62-year-old male can expect to live another 20.27 years, to age 82.27. At age 66, he may live another 17.37 years (to 83.37), and at 70, he could live on average 14.59 more years, to 84.59.

Females have a slightly longer lifespan for a variety of reasons. In addition, because women are often younger than their partners at the time of marriage, they tend to outlive their husbands. At 62 years old, a woman could expect to live another 23.14 years, to 85.14. At 66, she could live another 19.89 years, to 85.89. And at age 70, she may live another 16.75 years to the ripe age of 86.75.

Remember, this is not a crystal ball. No one can predict with certainty the year you will pass away. When making a realistic projection of your life expectancy, you should consider several factors, such as: how long people tend to live in your family; how healthy your own lifestyle is; what health conditions you already have; the amount of stress, anger, or worry in your life and how you are managing it; and whether you have healthy relationships or live a solitary life.

Some studies have shown that loneliness can have as much of a negative effect on your health as smoking 15 cigarettes a day! On the positive side, many of the factors just mentioned are under your control. Making healthy lifestyle changes may not only extend your life and your retirement benefits, but help you enjoy them much more as well.

ESTIMATING YOUR BENEFIT AMOUNT

The Social Security Administration has provided several ways to estimate your anticipated benefit amount long before you actually reach retirement age. Unfortunately, these different methods may produce very different results for reasons that are not always evident.

1. **Social Security Administration annual statement.** Anyone paying into the system can access their annual statement via the SSA website. However, the SSA only sends paper statements to those over 60 who aren't getting benefits and don't have a Social Security account set up online. Regardless of how you receive your statement, it does not specify whether the amounts are in today's dollars or in the inflation-adjusted dollars of the year you will start drawing benefits. It also assumes no growth in Social Security's Average Wage Index, although this has increased nearly every year since 1952.

2. **Over-the-phone or in-person estimates at an SSA office.** Staff will provide a benefit estimate but, like the SSA annual statement, may not tell you what year's dollar amount it is quoted in, or what assumptions, if any, the estimate makes regarding economic growth, inflation, or the Average Wage Index. If your quote is for an age over 65, they may reduce their quote by Medicare Part B premium payments and/or federal income tax withholding.

3. **Online benefits calculators.** Remarkably, the SSA provides four different online benefits calculators, but these vary in ease of use and accuracy. Don't be surprised if they generate four different numbers for you. You can find links to all these at https://PrepareforSocialSecurity.com/links.

- The Social Security Quick Calculator shows results both in today's dollars and future dollars (adjusted for cost of living).

- The Online Benefits Calculator requires a bit more work. You must input your earnings for every year you've worked.

- The Social Security Detailed Calculator requires even more work. You will have to download software to your computer and enter your year-by-year earnings history. On the plus side, it uses the most recent Cost of Living Adjustment to calculate your benefits.

- The Retirement Estimator requires you to provide identifying information, including your Social Security number, and finds your actual earnings to produce a benefit estimate.

Social Security benefits calculators should just be used as rough guides. Those that assume zero inflation and wage growth generate lower benefit estimates, especially for younger workers. This might help incentivize younger workers to set aside more for retirement to supplement Social Security.

They can also overestimate your future benefits by assuming that you will continue to earn what you currently do all the way to full retirement age.

In reality, if you move to lower-paying or part-time work *before* retirement, your benefit amount will likely be reduced. Why is this? Remember that your benefits are based on your 35 highest-earning years. If in your last few years before retirement, your income declines, it may lower your average income for those 35 years from what it would have been had you continued working full-time at a high-paying job. Note that working a part-time job *after* retirement has no negative impact on your benefits, unless you exceed the annual earnings limit set by the SSA.

MAXIMIZING BENEFITS IF YOU ARE MARRIED OR SINGLE

Some life situations will significantly impact your Social Security retirement strategy. Marriage and divorce, for example, open additional opportunities to maximize your family resources. **Keep in mind that any age difference or difference in earnings between you and your spouse needs to be taken into account before you decide that a given strategy is right for your situation.**

One popular approach is the "62/70 split." In this scenario, the spouse with lower earnings begins drawing Social Security at age 62, while the higher-earning spouse waits to file for benefits at age 70. This may help the family hedge their bets in terms of potential gains or losses due to life expectancy issues. Additionally, in the years the higher-earning spouse waits to draw Social Security, they have the option to start drawing a spousal benefit.

"Restricted Application" is another option for married couples. This tells the Social Security office that you are not both applying for all the benefits you are eligible for at the same time. This can be a way to claim a spousal benefit while allowing your own benefit to continue growing. This option is available if you were born on or before January 1, 1954, are eligible for a spousal benefit (including a benefit on an ex-spouse's earnings record), and you've reached full retirement age and have not yet claimed your own benefits.

If your benefit amount will be higher than the spousal benefit, you can switch to your benefit amount when you turn 70 years old. For those born on or after January 2, 1954, a restricted application may not be used for claiming spousal or ex-spousal benefits, but widows and widowers are eligible for restricted applications at any age. Further, someone caring for a child under age 16 or a disabled adult child may exercise an option to restrict the application to their spouse's benefits only, even if they have not yet reached their full retirement age.

Still another consideration is that the timing and amount of Social Security benefits you draw may bump you into another tax bracket. Anywhere from 50-85% of Social Security income may be taxable if it causes your Modified Adjusted Gross Income (MAGI) to reach certain thresholds. If this is your situation, you or your spouse might decide to delay drawing benefits or cut back on your work to keep your income at a level which you're not working simply to pay taxes and not enjoying the benefit of your labor.

Being single or married will not increase or decrease your personal retirement benefit because it is based on *your* earnings record. Each partner in a marriage collects their separate benefits based on their own work history. A spouse may receive spousal benefits based on their partner's work history, but this will not reduce the benefits the working partner receives themselves.

If a spouse passes away, the survivor becomes eligible for survivors benefits when they turn 60 (or 50 if the surviving spouse is disabled). However, if they remarry before reaching that age, they will lose that benefit from the deceased spouse's work record. If the *remarriage* ends by death or divorce, however, they can once again claim survivors benefits from their previous spouse who is deceased. But if they wait to get remarried until after 60 (or 50 if they are disabled), they will not lose their survivors benefit from the first spouse.

Be aware there is a maximum family benefit that limits how much Social Security a family can receive based on one retiree's work record. The limit is calculated based on benefits for retirement, disability payments, spousal, and children's benefits. It is generally equal to 150%-180% of the basic benefit rate. If the amount payable to family members exceeds this limit, the benefits will be reduced proportionately among all eligible family members. Benefits paid to a surviving divorced spouse based on disability or age will not count as part of this maximum amount.

MAXIMIZING BENEFITS IF YOU ARE DIVORCED

The rules for divorced spouses are similar for those who are separated by death, with a key difference being that anyone receiving benefits based on the work history of an ex-spouse will lose those benefits if they remarry, regardless of age. If you become single again due to death or divorce, you can begin collecting benefits based on your ex-spouse's work history again.

When divorced spouses are both still living at the time of retirement, your ex-spouse can draw Social Security calculated from your work record, even if you have remarried. This does not reduce the amount of Social Security you or your current spouse are entitled to. For an ex-spouse to claim these benefits, the marriage must have lasted at least ten years, the person making the claim must be unmarried and at least 62 years old, and the benefit they would receive based on their own earnings history must be less than what they would receive based on yours.

As long as you have been divorced for at least two years, your ex-spouse can receive benefits based on your earnings record, even if you have not yet applied for retirement benefits but can qualify for them. The SSA will pay the ex-spouse their own benefit and add to it an additional sum to bring it up to the full level of what they would have received from their partner if they had remained married.

An ex-spouse born before January 2, 1954 who has already reached full retirement age can, if they wish, elect to receive only the divorced spouse's benefit and wait until later to receive their own retirement benefit. However, for those born after this date, there is no longer the option to take only one benefit at full retirement age. Instead, if your ex-spouse files for one benefit, they will file for all retirement or spousal benefits.

THE DOUBLE-WHAMMY EFFECT

The "double-whammy effect" refers to the fact that some Social Security benefits are subject to taxation. This was a decision made by Congress in 1983 to prevent the Social Security Trust Fund from running out of money.

Many retirees find this tax galling because it feels like paying taxes twice on the same income—once when it was earned at work, and again when the benefits are received. It's worth noting that many retirees receive much more in benefits than the amount they contributed to the system over the years, but that doesn't make the tax any more palatable for those who are subject to it.

Moreover, the thresholds for taxation have never been adjusted for inflation. So as benefits increase over the years, a larger number of people are subject to the tax. In effect, this allows the government to tax more retirees and receive more revenue from each retiree without having to make the politically unpopular decision to vote to raise taxes on retirement.

For better or worse, here's how it works. The tax applies only after a retiree's income exceeds a threshold amount. It generally affects those with moderate or higher incomes. As of this writing, thirteen states also tax some or all of the Social Security benefits of their residents: Colorado, Connecticut, Kansas, Minnesota, Missouri, Montana, Nebraska, New Mexico, North Dakota, Rhode Island, Utah, Vermont, and West Virginia but make sure to check for the most up-to-date information (source: https://PrepareforSocialSecurity.com/sources).

At tax time, you have to add together your adjusted gross income, any municipal bond interest, and half of your Social Security benefits for the year. If this number is higher than $25,000 for an individual or $32,000 for a couple filing jointly, then up to 50% of your Social Security benefit must be added to your taxable income. If your base amount is more than $34,000 for an individual or $44,000 for a couple, you may be taxed on as much as 85% of your Social Security benefits. In either case, the base amount is $0 for people married but filing separately. They will have to pay tax on at least 50% of their benefits.

What does this mean for your decision about when to draw Social Security? It's mainly a concern for those who have other sources of retirement income, such as a traditional IRA or 401(k). One hundred percent of withdrawals from those investments are taxable, whereas only 50-85% of Social Security income is taxable. If you prefer to reduce your tax burden, you might want to consider drawing Social Security earlier rather than beginning to tap those types of investments. However, note that Roth IRA withdrawals are not taxable as they are funded with after-tax money.

SURVIVORS BENEFITS

What about survivors benefits? When a worker dies, their spouse, child, or parent may be eligible to apply for Social Security benefits based on their work record, if the deceased person worked long enough to qualify for benefits.

Workers can earn up to four Social Security credits each year. These are based on total wages and self-employment income for the year. The amount of earnings it takes to gain a credit can change each year. Consult the page "Social Security Credits" on the SSA website for the current year's income requirements. (You can find it via our Links page at https://PrepareforSocialSecurity.com.)

The younger the worker is, the fewer credits they have earned, reducing the amount available for survivors benefits. However, survivors may get benefits even if the worker has credit for only 1.5 years of work (six credits) in the three years prior to their death. This is especially important for very young widows or widowers who may think of Social Security as a benefit only available near retirement age.

The SSA will provide a one-time lump sum death payment of a whopping $255 to the surviving spouse or, if both spouses have passed away, the payment will be made to a child who is eligible for survivors benefits in the month of the worker's death. To receive this benefit, the beneficiary must have already been receiving benefits on the worker's record or became eligible for benefits upon the worker's death. If they are not yet eligible to receive Social Security benefits, they may still apply for this death payment within two years of their loved one's passing.

A widow or widower may receive benefits based on the deceased's earnings history if the survivor is 60 years old or more (50 or older if they have become disabled within seven years of the spouse's death), or at any age if they are not remarried and are the caregiver to the deceased person's child who is under 16 or has a disability. If the survivor remarries after age 60 (age 50 if you have a disability), the remarriage will not affect eligibility for survivors benefits from the prior marriage. If they wish, the survivor may switch to their own retirement benefit as early as age 62. If they are eligible for both survivors benefits and retirement benefits, they can choose to apply for one and switch to the other, higher benefit later.

A person who became eligible for retirement benefits less than 12 months before their spouse's death has the option to withdraw their retirement application and apply for survivors benefits only, then apply for retirement benefits later when they will be higher. Those already receiving retirement benefits when their spouse passes away can only apply for survivors benefits if the retirement benefit is less than the amount of survivors benefits. Applying for survivors benefits cannot be done online, but may be done by phone or by appointment at a Social Security office.

A surviving divorced spouse can receive benefits just like a widow or widower as long as the marriage lasted ten years or longer. These benefits will not reduce the amount for other survivors drawing benefits from the worker's earnings history, and they will not count against the family maximum that can be drawn based on that record. Even if the divorced spouse remarries, they will still be eligible for survivors benefits as long as they are at least 60 years old at the time of remarriage (50 if they have a disability).

Some special rules apply if the divorced spouse is caring for the former spouse's natural or legally adopted child who is under age 16 or has a disability. If the child is receiving benefits on the former spouse's record, the surviving divorced spouse does not have to meet the length-of-marriage rule. Moreover, if you are caring for your divorced spouse's child, *your* benefit does affect the amount of benefits available to others on the worker's record.

Children may receive Social Security benefits if they are unmarried. They must be younger than 18, up to 19 if they are a full-time elementary or high school student, or if they are older than 18 but have a disability that began before age 22. Stepchildren, grandchildren, step-grandchildren, and adopted children may also be eligible under certain circumstances.

If the parents of the deceased person depended on them for at least half of their support and are 62 or older, they may also be eligible for benefits. To receive benefits, the parents' own retirement benefits must not be higher than the benefit available on their child's work record. Moreover, the couple must not have married *after* the child's death, although there are some exceptions. Benefits are also available for stepparents or adoptive parents if they became parents before the child reached age 16.

The amount various survivors may receive is based on the earnings record of the person who died, the relationship of the survivor to the worker, their disability status, and the age at which they apply for survivors benefits. The chart below outlines what survivors benefits may look like for you:

Spouse or ex-spouse, full retirement age or older	100% of deceased worker's benefit amount
Spouse or ex-spouse, age 60	71.5% to 99%
Spouse or ex-spouse with disability, age 50-59	71.5%
Spouse or ex-spouse, any age, caring for a child under 16	75%
Child, under 18, or 19 if still in school or who has a disability	75%
One dependent parent, 62 or older	82.5%
Two dependent parents, 62 or older	75% each

SOCIAL SECURITY EXEMPTIONS

Some jobs are not subject to Social Security taxes, but if you take advantage of the exemption, you will not be able to receive any Social Security benefits. These are some of the exemptions:

Religious exemptions. You may claim a religious exemption from Social Security taxes if you are a member of a recognized religious group that is opposed to accepting Social Security benefits, including retirement and death or disability benefits. The group must have existed as of the end of 1950 and must have provided its members with a reasonable standard of living since then.

This is not an automatic exemption; you must claim it by filing Form 4029. If you have ever been eligible for Social Security benefits, the exemption is unavailable whether or not you actually received the benefit.

International exemptions. People who are not United States citizens or legal residents are considered nonresident aliens. Nonresident aliens who work in the United States typically pay Social Security tax on any income made in the country, even if they work for a foreign company. However, they are exempt if they work for a foreign government. Their families and domestic workers can also qualify for an exemption if they are also employed by the foreign government.

Foreign students and educators temporarily in the U.S. do not have to pay Social Security taxes. Depending on the type of visa the nonresident possesses, they may be eligible for the exemption.

Student exemptions. Students working for the school where they are enrolled, who receive employment because of their enrollment, may be exempt from paying Social Security taxes. This applies to money earned at the student's school, not wages earned from other employers.

Higher-earning exemption. There is a maximum income per year that the government may tax with Social Security. This means any income you earn that is greater than the maximum for the year is exempt from Social Security tax. The maximum is currently $147,000, but make sure to check for the most up-to-date information.

STEPS TO CONSIDER WHEN MAKING YOUR BIG DECISION

Here are a few steps to consider when making your decision about applying for Social Security benefits:

- ✓ Review the rules for when you qualify for full benefits and know your options.

- ✓ Use various Social Security retirement calculators to get a general idea of what your benefit amount might be if you retired at different ages. The longer you wait to retire, the higher your monthly benefit will be.

- ✓ Estimate your life expectancy, using the tool available on the SSA website, along with your own evaluation of your and your family's health history and lifestyle habits.

- ✓ Review your income sources and expenses, including pensions and any other retirement savings instruments you hold. Look through your budget (or create one if you haven't already!) to see how much you actually need to live on.

- ✓ Consider whether you are able and willing to work, and what kinds of work may be open to you.

- ✓ Think about what your surviving spouse will need to live on if you pass away first. What is their estimated life expectancy and health or disability status that may require substantial resources?

- ✓ Be honest with yourself: could you wait just one more year to start your Social Security benefits? Based on what you have learned so far in this book, waiting one more year could have a notable effect on your benefits, particularly if that means you will reach full retirement age or even age 70.

WORKING WHILE DRAWING BENEFITS

Many people erroneously believe you cannot work while drawing Social Security. This is a myth. In fact, when you do it, you and your family may actually increase your Social Security benefit. This is because every year your wages are reported to the SSA; they recalculate your benefits if your new year of work was one of your highest-earning 35 years, adjusted for inflation. There's no need to worry; if your work income while drawing Social Security isn't among your highest-earning years, it won't be counted against you.

The increase will be credited to you starting in January of the year after you earn these wages. Beginning with the month you reach full retirement age, your earnings will not reduce your benefits, no matter how much you earn.

Nevertheless, there are earnings limits for those who begin drawing benefits while they are younger than full retirement age. Those who are younger than full retirement age, and earn more than the annual earnings limit, may have their benefits reduced at a rate of $1 deducted from their benefit payments for every $2 they earn above the annual limit, which is currently nearly $20,000. In the year you reach full retirement age, the SSA deducts $1 in benefits for every $3 earned above a different limit, which is currently over $50,000. Earnings are only counted up to the month before you reach full retirement age, not your earnings for the whole year. Deductions from your benefits are calculated based on wages, bonuses, commissions, and vacation pay, but do not include pensions, annuities, investment income, interest income, veteran's benefits, or other government or military retirement benefits.

To better understand your individual situation when it comes to working while drawing benefits, use the SSA's Earnings Test Calculator. You can also consult the publication "How Work Affects Your Benefits," which explains in more detail the rules related to working while drawing Social Security. Both of these resources are available at https://PrepareforSocialSecurity.com/links.

SUMMARY OF HOW TO FILE FOR BENEFITS

Here's a basic summary of what you need to do to file for benefits, with more details to follow in later chapters.

1. Decide when you want to begin receiving benefits. You will find it helpful to set up a Social Security account at https://ssa.gov/myaccount. There, you can try out different retirement-age scenarios to see what your estimated benefits would be. You may also find the SSA's Retirement Planner helpful. You can find it here: https://PrepareforSocialSecurity.com/links.

2. Apply for benefits at least four months before the date you want them to start. For disability or survivors benefits, apply as soon as you are eligible at the SSA website. Based on which kind of benefit you want to apply for, you may have the option of applying online, in person at a Social Security office, or by phone. Although the online option may seem most convenient, filling it out without help from an SSA agent can result in errors that will delay the processing of your application and might cost you some benefits you are entitled to.

3. Provide the required documents. Coming to an appointment unprepared will cause you to have to return for another appointment and delay your application. Examples of documents you may need to apply for retirement benefits are:

   - Social Security number
   - Birth certificate (original or certified copy)
   - W-2 earnings statements or tax return from the previous year (photocopies are okay)
   - Military discharge papers (photocopies are okay)
   - Proof of U.S. citizenship or lawful alien status (original or certified copies)

4. Wait for a decision and work through the appeals process if you disagree with the amount or conditions of the benefits that have been offered to you.

HOW TO NAVIGATE THE SYSTEM

Navigating the Social Security system can be a challenge. Here is a list of suggestions to help you keep your sanity as you do so. We'll explore some of these in more detail in later chapters.

- Keep your records organized, with everything related to Social Security in the same place.
- Take careful notes on phone calls and office visits, including the dates of the conversations.
- Photocopy everything you mail to the SSA, and always attach your Social Security number to every document and letter you send.
- Do not send irreplaceable documents through the mail. Instead, hand-deliver them to a local Social Security office.
- Use the Social Security Administration website to find general answers to many questions, download forms, and get a rough idea of your eligibility and estimated benefits amounts.
- If you need assistance because of problems with the SSA or your own health issues, you may bring a companion with you when you meet with SSA representatives, and this person may also help you complete the application process.
- In the case of very difficult problems, especially with disability issues, hiring a lawyer who specializes in Social Security cases may be necessary.
- If you want to register a complaint with the Social Security Administration, feedback can be registered at the SSA website or on

a comment card at an SSA office. For more serious issues, you can contact your local SSA office in person or in writing, write to the national SSA office, contact your congressional representative for assistance, or secure the services of an attorney.

There are a lot of things to think about when deciding when and how to apply for Social Security benefits. The most important thing is to be aware of what benefits you are entitled to. **The Social Security Administration is not going to automatically enroll you into benefits for which you're eligible. You must take action!**

Many people simply don't know that they can draw Social Security on the work record of an ex-spouse or of a deceased spouse, parent, or child, for example. Once you know what you are entitled to, you can decide *when* it would be best to draw benefits. You can make this decision based on a level-headed estimation of your life expectancy and how the various options would affect your overall benefit as a family.

You and your spouse can also consider working during retirement if that is possible, desirable, and would improve your overall retirement picture. If it all seems confusing, well… it is! But the SSA has set up multiple ways to find the information you need and will allow you to use any helper you choose—a spouse, adult child, or trusted friend—to walk you through the process. Ultimately you can even hire a lawyer or appeal to lawmakers to help you with difficult issues.

There are many options for how to proceed. Work through them step by step at your own pace, and you'll get there, as millions have done before you.

CHAPTER THREE

SOCIAL SECURITY ELECTION CASE STUDIES

So far in this book, we've looked at Social Security from the 30,000-foot level, but it might not be clear how the rules apply in your specific case. No book can anticipate and answer every situation. Some cases are unique and complicated enough that you may need to hire a Social Security consultant or qualified financial advisor, accountant, or insurance agent to help you get the desired results. That investment could be well worth your money, both to get you the benefits you're entitled to and to save you the headache of going around in circles with the Social Security Administration to figure out the specifics.

However, there are some situations that come up frequently enough to warrant case studies to help you see how the rules might apply in your situation. We'll start with some strategies specifically for married couples, then look at scenarios that may affect both singles and married people.

SCENARIOS FOR MARRIED COUPLES

If you are married, you and your spouse have some important strategic decisions to make about when and how you will claim Social Security. Let's look at a few different situations:

1. **Claiming Social Security Early**

   Dale paid Social Security taxes for ten years, the minimum required to begin drawing benefits early, at age 62. Candace worked only nine years, so she was not able to draw Social Security based on her own earnings. However, she could collect on Dale's earnings record.

2. **Working Until Full Retirement Age**

   Tim and Wendy both waited until their full retirement age to begin drawing benefits. Wendy had worked more years than Tim and had a higher annual salary, so they decided to both collect benefits based on her work record. Since they waited until full retirement age, they received 100% of what they were entitled to.

3. **Working to the Maximum Retirement Age**

   Gary waited until he was 70 to retire, although he could have done so at his full retirement age of 67. This decision to work the maximum number of years resulted in him and his wife, Debbie, each receiving 124% of his retirement benefit.

4. **Using a Split Strategy**

   Andrew and Laura decided to use a split strategy. Laura had the lower earnings of the two of them, so she claimed her benefits at age 62 to help cover family finances. Andrew continued working at his higher income level until he was 70, then began drawing benefits. At that point, Laura switched her Social Security over to spousal benefits based on Andrew's work record.

SCENARIOS FOR BOTH SINGLE AND MARRIED PEOPLE

Whether you are single or married, here are a few scenarios that can apply either way.

CHAPTER THREE

SCENARIO 1: YOU GET A RAISE

As of this writing, the Social Security tax rate is 6.2% payable by the employee, and another 6.2% payable by the employer, for a total of 12.4%. If you are self-employed, you must pay the full 12.4% yourself, usually in quarterly payments due April 15, June 15, September 15, and December 15. (Note that the first quarterly payment is due in April, not March, to coincide with the federal and state income tax deadline.)

Currently, anyone with gross annual earnings between $400 and $147,000 is subject to this tax. Earnings less than $400 or more than $147,000 are not subject to Social Security tax. If you get a raise, your Social Security tax will be calculated based on your new gross income. You'll pay the same percentage, but the amount paid on a larger income will be higher.

Let's look at an example. Joey, Michelle, and Diego work for a lawn care business.

- ✓ Joey earned $40,000 last year. He paid 6.2% of this income, or $2,480, into Social Security ($40,000 x .062). His employer also paid 6.2% into Social Security for Joey. A total of $4,960 was paid into the system for his earnings that year.

- ✓ Michelle worked with Joey and started the year making the same income as him. Halfway through the year, she got a raise and ended up with a gross income of $45,000 for 2022. Just like Joey, she paid 6.2% of this income into Social Security. But because her gross income was higher, the amount she paid was $2,790 ($45,000 x .062). Her employer paid in the same amount, so the Social Security Administration collected $5,580 based on her earnings.

- ✓ Diego was a regional sales manager for the business. He expected to earn $147,000 last year, paying $9,114 to the SSA, with his employer matching this amount. However, near the end of the year, he scored a big sale and earned a commission of $10,000, bringing his gross income to $157,000 for the year. He and his employer still paid only $9,144 apiece into the system because $147,000 is the maximum taxable income for Social Security.

SCENARIO 2: A SPOUSE DIES

If your spouse passes away, you may be eligible for survivors benefits. However, you cannot draw both survivors benefits and your own Social Security retirement payment. When you are eligible for two benefits, Social Security pays you the higher of the two amounts. If you are already receiving a spousal benefit when your husband or wife dies, Social Security typically will automatically convert it to a survivor's benefit when the death is reported, and the deceased spouse was full retirement age. If the deceased spouse was under full retirement age, you must complete form SSA-4111 ("Certificate of Election for Reduced Widow(er)'s and Surviving Divorced Spouse's Benefit").

Here are a few scenarios:

- Susan was born between 1945 and 1956, so her full retirement age is 66. Her husband, Mark, died after she reached retirement age, so she qualifies for 100% of her husband's benefit amount.

- Jolynn is over 60 but had not yet reached her full retirement age when her husband, Mike, passed. She can draw 71.5% to 99% of her husband Mike's benefit.

- Jon was disabled in an accident that tragically took his wife JoJo's life. He is only 50, but because this is the minimum age a disabled person may draw benefits, he is able to draw 71.5% of his wife's benefit.

- Monica is only 34 years old, but she can draw 75% of Raj's benefit when he dies because they have a child who is under 16.

- Bill and Marcia have a 17-year-old daughter named Stephanie, who has a disability. When Marcia unexpectedly died, Bill was able to draw 75% of Marcia's benefit, even though he is only 43 years old, because he is caring for a disabled child.

SCENARIO 3: FILING AT DIFFERENT AGES

1. Filing early

- Because Elise was born in 1960, her full retirement age was 67. If she retires early, at 62, she will be entitled to only 70% of her retirement benefit. In this example: $700 a month.

2. Filing at full retirement age

- If Elise waits until her full retirement age of 67, she can receive 100% of her retirement benefit: $1,000 a month.

3. Filing at maximum retirement age

- Because she is in good health and can expect a longer average lifespan as a female, Elise decides to keep working until she is 70. At that point, she begins drawing $1,240 a month, or 124% of her Social Security benefit.

SCENARIO 4: YOU ARE WIDOWED OR DIVORCED

- Rashid was 60 years old when his wife, Anne, passed away. He can begin receiving reduced benefits right away. Once he reaches 62, he can claim his own early retirement benefits from Social Security if that amount is higher.

- Brittany was only 50 when her spouse, Kevin, passed. However, within seven years of his passing, she developed a disability, so she is able to receive survivors benefits. This would be true whether the disability developed seven years before or after Kevin's death.

- Richard started paying into Social Security when he was 18 but unfortunately passed away in an accident at the age of 28. Richard and his spouse, Mary, have a disabled daughter. Because Richard paid into Social Security for the minimum of ten years, Mary is able to draw Social Security based on his earnings in order to care for their daughter since she qualifies for child benefits.

- Jon and Amber divorced after a ten-year marriage. Amber died first, and Jon was able to draw benefits, the same as a widower. The benefits paid to him do not affect the benefit amount for other survivors drawing benefits on Amber's work record.

- Jon remarried Chelsea after he reached age 60. Because he waited until this age to get married, his remarriage does not affect his eligibility for survivors benefits based on Amber's earnings.

- Amber's second husband, Jack, also had a ten-year marriage to Amber before they divorced. He remarried when he was only 50, but he has a disability, so his remarriage also did not affect his eligibility for survivors benefits based on Amber's work record.

- Just before she died, Amber married Jason, and they adopted a disabled child. Although they were married less than ten years, because Jason is left caring for a disabled child, the length-of-marriage rule does not apply.

SCENARIO 5: YOU DECIDE TO WORK AN ADDITIONAL YEAR OR MORE

Working an additional year before retirement can greatly improve your financial picture. Even before considering Social Security benefits, that extra year gives you more time to save, more time for investment income to compound, another year of benefits covered by your employer, and one less year of retirement that you'll have to fund with savings.

In most cases, that extra year of work will also dramatically improve your Social Security picture. The Social Security Administration calculates your benefits based on an average of your 35 highest-earning years, so adding a higher-earning year will replace a lower-earning year in those calculations and raise your monthly benefit amount for life. And don't forget that the additional amount will be adjusted for inflation as well.

- Wendy has only 34 years of work in her earnings record. This means a zero will be averaged in for one missing year of work, lowering her average income and her monthly benefit amount. If she works one more year instead, she will replace that zero with a year of income and raise her monthly benefit.

- Tim had more than 35 years of work in his earnings record, but in some of his early years, his gross salary was quite low. By deciding to work one or more additional years at a higher income level, his new year(s) of work will replace the lowest of his 35 years, raising the average his monthly retirement benefits are based upon.

Working an additional year can also help you receive the total benefit amount you are entitled to.

- Full retirement age for Debbie was 66, and she was eligible to start drawing $1,500 a month, but she decided to work one more year. Because she did not claim her benefit until age 67, she now receives $1,620 per month. That extra $120 a month will give her another $1,440 per year for the rest of her life.

SCENARIO 6: CONTINUING TO WORK WHILE DRAWING BENEFITS

Even after beginning to draw Social Security retirement or survivor benefits, you can continue to work, and you may find that this actually brings you a higher benefit amount.

- Marty retired and began drawing benefits while continuing to work in his flower shop. In the previous year, his gross wages were one of the highest-earning 35 years of his working career. Because the SSA reviews the records of all Social Security beneficiaries who reported wages the previous year, Marty's benefits were recalculated, and he received an increased monthly benefit, payable retroactively to January of the year after he earned the money. If Marty's earnings were not higher than any of his 35 highest-earning years, then this would not decrease his monthly benefit amount.

- Seth decided to file for Social Security before reaching full retirement age and continue working. The annual earnings limit is currently $19,560. Seth's income was $29,570, or $10,000 more than the limit. The SSA deducted $1 from his benefits for every $2 he earned above his limit. This means Seth's benefits were reduced for the year by $5,000. Of course, because he earned a total of $10,000 more than the limit, this means he still came out $5,000 ahead for the year. If he needs the money badly, it may be worth it to him to, in effect, receive only 50% of his earnings over the limit.

- Millie waited until she reached full retirement age to claim her benefits, and she decided to keep working in her home business as well. In the year that she reached FRA, the Social Security Administration looked at her earnings for the months of that year before her birthday. If she passed the earnings limit for those months (which in 2022 was set at $51,960), her benefit will be reduced by $1 for every $3 over the limit she goes. So, if she goes $3,000 over the limit (earning $54,960) during those months, her benefit amount will be reduced by $1,000.

  Beginning with the month that Millie reached full retirement age, according to the rules, her earnings no longer reduced her benefits, no matter how much she earned. With this knowledge in mind, Millie decided to cut back on her work hours and just enjoy some vacation time with her family in the months leading up to her birthday to stay under the $51,960 limit. After her birthday, she began working extra hours in her business and pushed her income above $100,000 for the year. This did not reduce her Social Security benefits at all.

SCENARIO 7: YOU ARE A FEDERAL WORKER OR ARE NOT ELIGIBLE FOR SOCIAL SECURITY

Here are some examples of people in special categories who may not be eligible for Social Security benefits:

- Laurie started working for the federal government in the early 1980s. As a federal employee hired before 1984, she was included in the Civil Service Retirement System and did not have Social Security taxes deducted from her paychecks. Therefore, she is not eligible for Social Security benefits.

- Jenny only worked for nine years outside the home and paid Social Security taxes. Because she had not accrued the required 40 credits (about ten years of wages), she is not eligible for Social Security based on her own earnings. However, if she decides to work one additional year, she will be able to draw benefits.

- Marina died at age 61. Because she had not yet reached the minimum retirement age of 62, she was unable to draw Social Security benefits. Her husband was not yet 60 when she died. However, once he reached 60, he was able to start drawing survivors benefits. Had he been disabled, he could have drawn benefits as early as age 50.

- Andrew and Laura were American citizens who had traveled quite a bit in the former Soviet Union and wanted to retire there. They knew that historically the United States had placed restrictions on Social Security payments to people in this country and in the separate independent countries that had emerged from the breakup of the U.S.S.R. They used the SSA's "Payments Abroad Screening Tool" and found there were no restrictions on U.S. citizens receiving

Social Security payments in Estonia, although it was a former Soviet republic, and decided to retire there. (See https://PrepareforSocialSecurity.com/links for the Screening Tool.)

- Amos is a member of the clergy. He filed IRS Form 4029 with the Social Security Administration to claim a religious exemption from participating in the system. Upon approval, he did not pay Social Security taxes and is not eligible to draw benefits. This applies whether he is classified as an employee of his organization or as a self-employed individual contracted by the organization.

- Bradley has at least ten years of service in the railroad industry (or at least five years after 1995), so his benefits are covered through the Railroad Retirement Board (RRB), an independent federal agency that administers benefits for railroad employees and their families. He is not eligible for Social Security benefits.

- Frank, Bradley's co-worker, has less than ten years of service in the railroad industry (or less than five years after 1995). He does not receive RRB benefits. Instead, his account is transferred into Social Security, and he will be eligible for benefits after meeting the Social Security benefit requirements.

- Mindy was self-employed and should have paid self-employment taxes sufficient to cover both her own and the employer's portions of Social Security contributions. However, she did not report her income and evaded paying taxes on it. When she is ready to retire, she will not receive any benefits because there is no record of her paying anything into the system.

- Rosalinda immigrated to the United States when she was already close to retirement age and did not have the 40 U.S. work credits needed to qualify for Social Security benefits. Her country has a "totalization agreement" with the United States. As a result, she was able to earn six work credits in the U.S. and receive prorated benefits as well as prorated benefits from her home country.

- Sven also immigrated to the United States as an adult near retirement age. He worked long enough in his home country to receive retirement benefits from them, and his country's laws allowed him to receive benefit payments while living abroad. He does not receive United States Social Security benefits, but receives his benefits from his home country and lives on them during his American retirement.

FOUR POSSIBLE DIRECTIONS

Social Security can be so complicated, it's tempting just to trust what the Social Security Administration tells you rather than going through the hassle of proving you deserve more. Even an increase of $100 a month in your benefits adds up over the years. When you're in retirement, every dollar will count. A little extra trouble on the front end can make your life easier later.

If you pore over the Social Security website and other online sources, and still are confused, what can you do next? There are four possible directions you can go for answers: the SSA offices, a lawyer, a financial planner, or a Social Security consultant. Let's look at the pros and cons of each of these.

1. SOCIAL SECURITY ADMINISTRATION EMPLOYEES

- Their assistance is free of charge.
- They do this full-time, so they are in a better position than most to give an accurate answer.
- They have different levels of representatives: Service Representatives, Claims Representatives, and Technical Experts who can deal with increasingly complex problems.

- **The SSA is understaffed and overworked. The knowledge levels of representatives may differ widely.**

- They are not allowed to give advice or recommendations, but some invariably do.

- You may get different answers from different employees and from different tools on the website.

- Employees have a lot of problems to solve. They may not be highly motivated to track down the better options for you if you are satisfied with the first thing they tell you.

2. LAWYERS

- A lawyer works for you rather than for the government and may be more highly motivated to help you.

- A lawyer who specializes in Social Security may be more knowledgeable about certain areas of it than a less-experienced SSA representative.

- Attorneys are expensive. You have to weigh whether the cost will be worth the possible increase in your benefits.

- Many Social Security attorneys only specialize in Social Security disability benefits and are paid on a contingency basis. If they win the case, they receive a portion of your past-due disability benefits. If you aren't trying to file for Social Security disability, you may have to contact several before finding one who will work for you on an hourly basis or who can help with Social Security retirement advice.

3. FINANCIAL PLANNERS

- Some financial planners offer their advice for "free."
- Like a lawyer, a financial planner works for you rather than the SSA, so they may be more incentivized to track down the best deal for you.

- It can be difficult to find a financial planner with a thorough knowledge of Social Security.
- Planners who offer their services for "free" will often try to sell you mutual funds, stocks, life insurance, annuities, or other products that will make a fee or commission for them.

4. SOCIAL SECURITY CONSULTANTS

- They are usually certified by one of the two major certification organizations and typically have worked at the SSA or in tax, law, or financial planning.
- They have experience and can make recommendations when you give them information about your lifestyle and financial situation. The more detailed information you share, the better the outcomes.

- ✓ They ask lots of questions and do not take a one-size-fits-all approach. They help you consider lifestyle and financial information to create a personalized plan.

- ✓ They can actually assist you, in person or with filing online, or help you understand what to do and when to do it.

CONS 👎

- ✓ Consultants can be expensive.

- ✓ It is hard to know if their advice is sound because there are no common "standards" within this space to hold consultants accountable.

- ✓ They are not fiduciaries, so you need to interview them in detail in order to determine if they are qualified to help you.

Hopefully, these practical scenarios help you see some of the real-life implications the Social Security rules can have on people in different situations. Even if your situation is similar to one described here, you should follow up with your own investigation online, with SSA personnel, and if necessary, with an attorney, Social Security consultant (you can find this service on https://PrepareforSocialSecurity.com), or a qualified financial advisor. What I've provided here can be a good starting point for your investigation.

CHAPTER FOUR

THE "FRUSTRATING FLAWS" OF SOCIAL SECURITY

As we set the stage for this chapter, let's look at a few pieces of information to help us grasp how critical Social Security is for families in the United States.

Nearly all workers in the United States contribute to Social Security, and the vast majority of adults are eligible for benefits. Social Security payments help lift over a million children above the poverty line. For a young family with two children, it is the equivalent of having a life insurance policy with a face value of nearly $800,000.

Without Social Security, four out of ten adults 65 and older (16 million people) would fall below the poverty line. It provides half the income of 50% of people in this age group, and for 25% of this group, it provides 90% of their income (source: https://PrepareforSocialSecurity.com/sources).

The importance of the program makes its problems all the more frustrating. However, we don't have the option of throwing up our hands and saying, "forget it" just because it can be difficult to navigate. In this chapter, we'll explore some of the most frustrating flaws of Social Security and what you can do about them. Under each flaw, I'll elaborate on the problem as well as offer a potential solution.

1. YOUR SOCIAL SECURITY BENEFITS ARE TAXED.

Problem: If you have little or no income other than Social Security, you generally will not be taxed on your benefits. However, the threshold for paying taxes on Social Security benefits is low.

Individuals with a total gross income of at least $25,000 or couples filing jointly with a gross income of at least $32,000 will be taxed on up to 50% of their Social Security income. For individuals with a combined gross income of $34,000 or a couple filing jointly with a combined gross income of at least $44,000, up to 85% of their benefits would be taxable.

As of this writing, there are thirteen states that tax some or all of their residents' Social Security benefits. These are: Colorado, Connecticut, Kansas, Minnesota, Missouri, Montana, Nebraska, New Mexico, North Dakota, Rhode Island, Utah, Vermont, and West Virginia but make sure to check for the most up-to-date information.

Solution: Consult a tax advisor to plan carefully when you and your spouse will claim benefits and how long either or both of you will continue working. In some cases, you may find that it's better to quit your job than to allow it to push you over the threshold of owing taxes.

In other situations, the income you receive will be substantially more than what you pay out in taxes, so you may find it worthwhile. This calls for careful thought and planning. If you're going to work for free, wouldn't you rather volunteer that time for a cause you believe in?

Before making a move to another state, consider the tax implications. **You might save yourself a lot of money over the years by simply choosing which side of a state border to live on.**

2. THE SOCIAL SECURITY ADMINISTRATION IS NOT OBLIGATED TO REMIND YOU TO FILE FOR BENEFITS.

Problem: The Social Security Administration has no obligation to track down every taxpayer as they reach retirement age and remind them to file for benefits. This means some people who are entitled to benefits may continue working when they could retire. Or they may never file for benefits at all and lose what they have paid into the system.

In most cases, adult children or friends will remind the older person and help them navigate the filing process if necessary. But those who are unaware, unable, or don't have people in their life to help them can fall through the cracks and live in unnecessary poverty.

You also need to know specifically what benefits you're applying for and provide all the necessary information to receive them. If you're divorced, your benefits might be higher if you claim them against your ex-spouse's work record rather than yours. If you have a disability, you may qualify for additional benefits. If a worker passes away, survivors might qualify for benefits—if they apply for them.

Solution: After reading this book, you should have an understanding of the basics of filing for Social Security benefits. If you use an online or print calendar, why not jump ahead to the year you become eligible and create a reminder for yourself? Talk to your spouse and children so they know your plan and can help remind you as the time draws closer.

You can also keep a monthly budget in a spreadsheet or on paper. That's another great place to post a reminder to yourself so you can anticipate how your Social Security benefits will affect your monthly budget.

3. MILLIONS OF PEOPLE WORK BUT AREN'T COVERED BY SOCIAL SECURITY.

Problem: We've already seen that there are whole categories of people who will not be eligible for Social Security benefits when they retire. This includes but is not limited to:

- People who have not worked long enough to earn the necessary income credits.
- People who have not paid Social Security taxes.
- Immigrants who have not worked in the United States long enough.

- Some categories of federal workers and some railroad workers.
- Clergy who have opted out of the system for religious reasons.

In such situations, even if a person applied at their retirement age, they would be denied because they have not paid into the system. Social Security is not a form of welfare. It is a form of insurance purchased by the worker and their employers and guaranteed by the federal government. Therefore, if you haven't met the criteria to purchase it, you won't receive it.

Solution: Those who fall into the above categories need to look at their options for alternative funding for their retirement. These could include things like participating in employer 401(k) plans; independently investing in IRAs, mutual funds, individual stocks and bonds, annuities or insurance policies; or acquiring and renting out or selling real estate.

For homeowners in areas where homes have appreciated in value or have low mortgage balances, downsizing to a smaller house in a less expensive area may yield a substantial nest egg from the equity of their previous home. Some people achieve similar results with a reverse mortgage.

For people without these options, working, drawing public assistance, or receiving support from family members may help them make ends meet. All these options are beyond the scope of this book. The main point is to know whether or not you will be able to draw Social Security and to make proactive plans for the living expenses you will have during retirement.

4. THE PROGRAM IS COMPLICATED AND BUREAUCRATIC.

Problem: The basic framework of the Social Security program has not changed greatly since its inception, but the various interlinked programs within it and the many exceptions to the rules can be quite complex. To give you an idea of just how complex it is, SSA representatives are considered "trainees" for their first three years on the job! Despite having tens of thousands of employees, the SSA struggles to help citizens navigate their own bureaucracy. It's not unusual to get a busy signal on the phone or encounter an inexperienced or poorly-informed employee.

Solution: Millions of people successfully apply for Social Security and draw benefits. In fact, payment accuracy has been estimated at over 99%. This may be small comfort if you are among those with an extraordinary situation that calls for a more in-depth study of the rules. But if you are patient and persistent, you can get the help you need. Otherwise, you can always engage or hire a professional to help you navigate the system.

5. THE SOCIAL SECURITY ADMINISTRATION MAY PROVIDE INACCURATE AND INCONSISTENT ANSWERS.

Problem: The Social Security Administration has done its best to sort through extraordinarily complicated rules with numerous exceptions. It has also tried to make the information available in a user-friendly format on the SSA website. For basic questions, they've done a pretty good job. The site is relatively easy to use, and you can find simple answers quickly.

The problem comes when you have a special situation that is out of the ordinary. The SSA does not have nearly enough staff to give each person the detailed attention they need. With high staff turnover, you might find yourself talking with someone who is fairly new to the job and anxious to resolve your problem quickly so they can move on to the next person. Moreover, the website provides several different calculators to help you figure out how much your benefits will be. Each of these can yield wildly different answers for you, with no clear explanation of why they are so different.

Solution: If the person you are speaking with seems inexperienced or uncertain, make notes on what they say. Then speak to a different representative on the phone or make an appointment, at a different office if necessary, to see if you get a similar answer. Even if you are highly capable of handling this yourself, it may be wise to take along a second adult to help take notes and ask questions to make sure there are no misunderstandings.

If the issue is particularly serious and you're not getting clear answers, this might be the time to engage a private Social Security consultant or attorney. Remember that if you disagree with the SSA's decisions about your benefits, you have the right to go through a couple of levels of appeals that will get your case seen by other people at higher levels who will give it more in-depth attention.

6. THE RULES ALLOW MOST PEOPLE TO TAKE SOCIAL SECURITY TOO SOON.

Problem: People are much healthier and live much longer today than when Social Security was initially set up. This means the earlier you retire, the longer your benefits have to sustain you. Most people continue to work after beginning to draw their benefits. Many healthy people begin drawing benefits at the earliest possible date out of fear the program will not last or an expectation that this will give them more money altogether than if they wait and start drawing larger checks by accepting a later retirement date.

Let's be honest. The government likely wants you to take your benefit early because it means they will have to pay out less money–which means you get less money. If their goal was to ensure you actually enjoy the maximum amount of benefits, they wouldn't even allow for the possibility of electing early. It saves the government around 8% of your benefits for every year early you take Social Security before your full retirement age.

Unless you are in poor health or have a family medical history that suggests your lifespan will be shorter than normal, it is generally advantageous *for individuals* to wait as long as possible to start receiving Social Security. *For married couples,* there are situations where it is advantageous for the lower-earning spouse to file at 62, while the higher-earning spouse files at 70.

Solution: This is where it's so important to be well-educated about the system so you can make rational decisions rather than emotional ones. A misguided decision can cost you a large portion of your hard-earned retirement. Of course, there are some situations in which drawing benefits early is the best choice. It's a good idea to speak with a Social Security consultant or qualified financial advisor about your individual situation to help you make the best possible decision for you.

7. LUMP SUM BENEFITS CREATE SPECIAL PROBLEMS.

Problem: Some people decide not to begin their benefits at full retirement age, but later change their minds. This can happen for any number of reasons, including just being confused about their options at first and learning more later, or being convinced by a friend or family member that they need to reverse their decision. In addition, a change in their financial situation might make them feel they need to begin drawing their benefits immediately.

The individual could then request from the SSA to start their benefits retroactively and receive in a lump sum up to six months' worth of benefits (or less, depending on how many months have passed since they reached full retirement age). Doing so will reduce the amount of their future benefits because they will not receive the higher amount they were due from having delayed their retirement.

One of the biggest problems that comes from taking a lump sum is that it can push you into a higher tax category, making more of your income subject to taxation. If your income exceeds $85,000, your Medicare Part B and Part D premiums may also temporarily increase due to IRMAA (you can learn more about IRMAA by searching for the topic on Matt's Corner Blog at https://PrepareforMedicare.com/blog). And we haven't even mentioned the disruptive effects on a family budget of getting a large one-time infusion of cash.

As welcome as this might seem, in many cases, it creates a temptation to make large impulse purchases or, at the very least, gives you an unrealistic idea of what kind of lifestyle you will be able to afford in retirement. Thus, it sets you up for disappointment and possible future financial problems.

Solution: The six-month rule is a nice safety measure in case you make a decision you later come to regret, but it's far preferable to research and think carefully about your decision in the first place and stick to it. Remember, it's your money, your life, and your decision. Don't feel pressured by SSA representatives, friends, or adult children to make a decision you don't understand or don't think is wise.

If you do decide to take a lump sum, talk to your tax professional about how it will affect your tax liability and ways you can offset this. For some people, this might mean taking a leave of absence from work or quitting a part-time job to keep their annual income from going too high. If you itemize, you might have some options for offsetting some income with charitable donations. If you were considering starting a small business, some income could be offset by business expenses.

These suggestions are outside the scope of this book, but they might give you an idea of some of the questions you could ask a tax professional.

8. MONTHLY PAYMENTS ARE LOW.

Problem: Average monthly Social Security payments are above the poverty level and successfully keep millions of seniors out of poverty. However, they are still too low for many people to maintain the same lifestyle they have become accustomed to before retirement. Many people experience a drop in their standard of living when they rely mostly on Social Security.

Solution: Remember that Social Security benefits were never intended to be your only source of income in retirement. It's best to consider them as a base on which you will layer other kinds of retirement income, such as pensions, investments, rental income, or part-time work.

9. MANY DECISIONS ARE NOT REVERSIBLE.

Problem: The decisions you make can have a costly effect on your Social Security benefits. For example, after you file for your retirement benefit, you forfeit the right to file for any other benefit, such as disability. Another example might be taking your retirement benefit before age 70, which will reduce the survivors benefits your spouse will receive.

If you get divorced even just one day before your tenth wedding anniversary, neither you nor your ex-spouse will be able to receive spousal or survivors benefits. A decision to get remarried will also cost you those benefits from your first spouse. If you make a mistake in filing for retirement benefits and change your mind, you have one year to withdraw your benefit, repay everything you received, and start again. If you wait one day past the deadline, you are stuck with your decision.

Solution: These problems can all be solved by becoming well-informed about the rules of Social Security and being intentional and strategic in your planning. Of course, decisions such as marriage and divorce often happen much earlier in life when few people are giving Social Security much thought. But if you are headed into the unfortunate situation of divorce, and you're aware of the rules, you will need to be aware that it will have an impact on your Social Security earnings. That is not necessarily a reason to stay married, but if you are well-informed, you can make an educated decision about the pros and cons of staying married versus getting divorced.

10. THE SOCIAL SECURITY SYSTEM IS VULNERABLE TO POLITICAL DEADLOCKS.

Problem: Social Security touches the lives of nearly every American citizen. Powerful political interests battle over it, but ultimately, it would not be in a politician's self-interest to try to abolish this program. On the other hand, political deadlocks in Washington that paralyze the government from doing basic things like passing a budget also prevent meaningful reforms that could put the Social Security system on a more stable foundation to serve American citizens better.

Solution: No one exactly knows how to solve this problem, but from the perspective of the average person, it's not necessary that the entire program be fixed, right? What's necessary for you and me is that we are able to receive the benefits we have worked for. We can have peace of mind on this issue—not because we think Washington will get it sorted out, but because we know that they will not likely be able to abolish the program or significantly reduce it for people who are retiring soon.

Yes, future generations may see reduced benefits and will need to find additional ways to supplement their incomes. We should talk to our children and grandchildren and encourage them to take appropriate steps for their own financial future. But there is no need for us to worry, panic, or reduce our benefits by taking them prematurely.

11. THE FILING STRATEGY FOR MARRIED PEOPLE IS COMPLICATED.

Problem: Social Security offers married people a lot of different options, including filing at different ages from one another and deciding whether to base your benefits on your own income or your spouse's. It becomes even more complicated in situations of divorce, disability, or death. Couples who are not aware of the benefits available to them or do not receive knowledgeable advice may miss out on many tens of thousands of dollars they have earned.

Solution: For many couples, finances can be a source of conflict. Making decisions together about Social Security may be especially challenging because it involves comparing our past earnings records and making once-in-a-lifetime decisions that will determine our monthly benefits for the rest of our lives. It's important at this time not to devalue the contributions of the lower-earning spouse, who may have gaps in their work record because they contributed to the family in other ways, such as raising children and maintaining a household.

While acknowledging and respecting one another's emotions, it's important to make decisions about Social Security rationally. One spouse may wish to delay retirement because that seems to them a sign of "growing old." Or another may be looking forward to retirement and wish to file first to make it official.

Instead, couples are well-advised to read up on different strategies that will maximize their income and enable them to live the kind of life they want during retirement. If the choices seem overwhelming, this would be a good area to bring in the advice of a professional Social Security consultant or qualified retirement planner.

WHAT'S THE POINT?

Maybe you have found this chapter to be a little scary. It may have raised issues you hadn't thought about, or given you more to worry about. That's not the point of it, though. I want you to come away from this chapter with two main pieces of knowledge:

1. I want to make you aware of some of the danger areas that may cost you money if you don't make thoughtful, well-informed decisions.

2. I want to reassure you that for each of these danger areas, there are some practical things you can do to take care of yourself and your family instead of living in worry or fear.

Look back over your life and think of all you've accomplished. What was life like when you were a child? How did you get by then without all the conveniences we have today? Remember what school was like? Remember the stress you had studying for exams? What about relationships and the joy and heartbreak they brought? Was it easy to build your career? What kinds of sacrifices did you make to support your family, buy a house, pay for necessities, and have a few memorable luxuries? If you raised kids, how easy was that? Can you trace any gray hairs back to that experience?

Friend, you have been through a lot, and you have done well. Even if everything didn't turn out exactly as you'd planned, you learned, experienced, and grew. You came out on the other side wiser. You got through some really tough times in life, and you're still going strong today.

So, when it comes to your retirement benefits and all the aggravation and problems you might see in the process of getting the rewards you've worked for, just keep in mind that you have overcome far worse problems in your life. This is actually small potatoes compared to some of what you've been through. And just as you found a way back then, again and again, to get through each new challenge, you'll find your way through the challenge of retirement.

CHAPTER FIVE

THE SOCIAL SECURITY MARKETING MACHINE

We all know Social Security can be confusing. You'd assume that all the information available out there would automatically help. However, it can be both an advantage and a disadvantage. The answers you need are out there, but it can take quite a bit of research to find the diamond you need in a field full of pebbles.

You can appreciate the friends or relatives who may help you out of the goodness of their hearts, but they will not be as knowledgeable about the complexities of the system as professionals are. Conversely, some "professionals" may not be able to prove their Social Security advice or consulting qualifications. Others may give generic advice, only to move quickly beyond Social Security advice and into selling other products without really digging into your specific Social Security plan.

"Forearmed is forewarned," though. So, in this chapter, I want to "forearm" you with knowledge about the Social Security marketing machine and how you can make it work in your favor.

DIFFERENT AVENUES OF MARKETING

First, let's look at how the government gets free information about Social Security out to the public. Then we'll look at how private businesses market Social Security information and services.

One of the primary ways the government publicizes information about Social Security to the general public is through the official https://www.ssa.gov website. Depending on the level of detail, you can find what you need quickly on the website—or not. It's a government website for an absolutely massive federal program, so of course, it can be clunky. It's not surprising to find some parts of the site have been updated, and others haven't, or different pages of the site may give conflicting information.

In addition to their website, the SSA also communicates Social Security information through social media. The Social Security Administration has accounts on both Twitter (https://twitter.com/SocialSecurity) and Facebook (https://facebook.com/SocialSecurity), which are used to promote their services through various links to their website.

The SSA also apparently has a marketing budget. It seems odd that the Social Security Administration (and Medicare, for that matter) is allowed to spend taxpayer money on advertising campaigns through social media ads, email, YouTube videos, billboards, and posters at bus stations and other mass transit sites.

Private businesses use many of the same techniques as the government. Many financial advisors will market Social Security assistance through Facebook and other social media platforms.

One way they do this is to sponsor targeted ads that entice people to learn more about upcoming changes, followed by ads for a "free" seminar to explain the changes. Many private businesses run smaller, more localized marketing campaigns than the government. Social media ads can be targeted to very specific demographics, even within just a one-mile radius of a residential location; can offer timely messages related to very recent changes; and can be customized for the needs and interests of a particular community—for example, a high number of veterans in a military town.

While these companies can offer assistance, there are very strict laws addressing misleading advertisements. This means businesses can't give the impression that they represent or are affiliated, endorsed, or approved by the Social Security Administration or the Centers for Medicare & Medicaid Services (Medicare).

Be aware that many services, such as correcting Social Security cards, replacing lost cards, getting a Social Security statement, or getting a new number for a child, are available free of charge from the government, even though some businesses charge a fee to help you.

Some companies also provide information and consultation services, which are marketed in similar ways. Because they might have larger advertising budgets and public awareness, they are able to optimize for search engines more easily and be seen by a larger, more national audience. Some companies specialize in training other firms how to provide Social Security advice without running afoul of government regulations.

WHAT TO LOOK OUT FOR

With so many potential sources of information, it is hard to determine which ones are reliable. Information can come from blogs, news articles or videos, magazine articles, or individual websites. On top of all of it, social media frequently links to any and all of those sources, confusing matters even further.

That's precisely why I launched the companion to this book and workbook, https://PrepareforSocialSecurity.com. There, you'll find a Helpful Links section that cuts through much of the clutter and forwards you to real sites, a blog to keep you up-to-date with your Social Security, as well as an opportunity to explore Social Security consulting services.

As with any topic, there are a few key elements to look for when selecting sources of information about Social Security. A popular approach many universities teach their students for evaluating research sources can be helpful to us here. Just remember CRAAP!

C: CURRENCY

Currency refers to the timeliness of the source. A blog post or news article from ten years ago, for instance, is not likely to be a reliable source because some Social Security rules and figures change from year to year. If a source of information does not list a date, take it with a grain of salt. Most of the better sources at least tell you when they were last updated, which helps ensure their accuracy and usefulness.

R: RELEVANCE

How important is the information to your needs? With something as large and complex as Social Security, it is vital to sort through the mountain of information to find what actually applies. This can be tough to do on SSA.gov. Certain programs and guidelines may only apply to a certain portion of the population, yet may be presented by some sources to apply to everyone, making them less helpful to you. Search specifically for the information you need. You don't need to master the whole system, just the parts that apply to you.

A: AUTHORITY

It makes sense that the most-used website about Social Security is the official website, https://www.ssa.gov. Any other websites ending in ".gov" are also largely accurate, though many will point back to the Social Security Administration's website. In my experience, state government-based websites are less accurate. Other websites may contain good information, but should be double-checked against primary sources, which are more likely to be more accurate. Private blogs or social media posts may not be updated on a regular basis.

A: ACCURACY

How true and correct is the information you've found? Confirming information against that listed on https://www.ssa.gov is a good way to check accuracy. Additionally, if one source is giving information that is wildly different than all the other sources, something is wrong.

This is one reason why it is vital to consult multiple sources before making any significant decisions on Social Security or coming to any life-altering conclusions. Corroboration by multiple sources often means greater accuracy since there can be legal penalties for falsifying this information for personal or corporate gain.

P: PURPOSE

With any source of information, you must examine why the information is being presented. The information on https://www.ssa.gov is there as a public service to help the constituents, not to turn a profit or to get you to buy some other product. Information on a financial advisor's personal blog or Facebook page is likely there to drive business for the advisor.

When you see an article with an alarming headline warning about significant changes to the system without clearly stating what those changes are, it could be advertising or "clickbait." Clickbait is a term internet advertisers use to describe headlines designed to make you panic and take action by clicking on the article, and hopefully the advertisements surrounding the article. Anything too good to be true, especially when stated by a suspicious website, likely is.

One of the best safeguards is to consult multiple sources. Though the Social Security Administration website is likely your best choice, this doesn't mean it is guaranteed to be reliable, easy to find topics, or use. At times there may be a lag in updating information with very recent changes to the program, or updates may be made in one part of the website but not in another area that touches on the same issues. Furthermore, with anything we read, we might just misunderstand a particularly confusing passage and find that other sources can help clarify it.

Some of the more reliable non-governmental websites you might want to compare include:

- Prepare for Social Security: https://PrepareforSocialSecurity.com
- The Center for Retirement Research at Boston College: https://crr.bc.edu

Social Security Works (an advocacy organization): https://socialsecurityworks.org

HOW TO AVOID SCAMS

There are only a few ways the Social Security Administration will contact people, and only certain things they will do. According to their website, "We use emails, text messages, and social media to provide information on our programs and services. However, we will not request personal or financial information through these methods. Sometimes, we send emails with information that is particular to your needs, usually after a discussion with you in person or over the phone. When we make phone contact, it is often to confirm the legitimacy of claims."

They will never threaten you, suspend your Social Security number, or demand immediate payment from you. They will never require payment by retail gift card, wire transfer, cryptocurrency, or mailing cash. They will never promise a benefit increase or other assistance in exchange for payment.

Here are a few of the more common Social Security scams you might encounter:

 Fraudulent phone calls, sometimes by a human or sometimes by an artificial robotic voice. Typically, they will pretend to represent the SSA and may use technology to spoof the actual SSA phone number to trick your caller ID. Sometimes the call is friendly, offering services such as enrolling a new member, providing a Social Security card, or providing records of contributions to Social Security. The SSA actually provides these services for free, but scammers will try to get you to pay a fee for them or divulge sensitive personal information.

Other scammers will take a threatening tone, telling you that you could be sued or arrested if you don't pay some kind of fee or provide your Social Security number and other identifying information. Of course, the goal of getting this information is identity theft. Rest assured, the

SSA rarely, if ever, makes phone calls to clients unless you have some kind of ongoing business you've been trying to work out with them. And if, for some reason, the actual Social Security Administration phoned you about something important, they would follow up with other means of communication if you didn't take their call.

- **Fraudulent text messages,** attempting to scare the recipient by claiming there is a problem with their Social Security number and that they should call a help number. From there, scammers will attempt to collect personal information.

- **Fraudulent emails,** often appearing to be actual messages, resembling authentic letters, and including the seal and font styles of the SSA. Some may even redirect recipients to fake web pages. Again, their goal is to obtain personal information. Authentic SSA emails will never seek personal information.

- **Fraudulent direct mail,** like the others, threatening to suspend benefits unless a certain number is called to provide personal information.

The SSA also shares the following warning signs to look out for:

- The caller or sender says there is a problem with your Social Security number or account.

- Any call, text, or email asking you to pay a fine or debt with retail gift cards, wire transfers, prepaid debit cards, internet currency, or by mailing cash.

- Scammers pretending they are from Social Security or another government agency. Caller ID, texts, or documents sent by email may look official, but they are not.

- Callers threaten you with arrest or other legal action.

What exactly can you do to protect yourself?

- ✓ Do not return unknown calls, emails, or texts.
- ✓ Do not share your personal identifying information, such as your Social Security number, date of birth, or bank account details, by email, text, or over the phone.
- ✓ Do not send anyone money or make major financial decisions without first asking for input from someone you trust.
- ✓ If you receive a questionable call, hang up and report it at <u>oig.ssa.gov</u> (Office of the Inspector General).

When it comes to protecting yourself, it's not enough just to avoid scams. It's also incredibly helpful to have some awareness of how marketing companies target you as the consumer. After all, it's no accident that you're seeing those specific advertisements! It's all part of a carefully orchestrated effort to target just the right customers.

HOW TO USE THE MARKETING MACHINE IN YOUR FAVOR

So far in this chapter, you've learned about different avenues of marketing, a few items to note when evaluating sources of Social Security information, and how to avoid scams. But I don't want you to live in fear. To take it a step further, I want to encourage you to turn the "marketing machine" on its head and use it in your favor. Here are a few suggestions.

First and foremost, take advantage of all the information already coming your way. You've probably gotten pieces of direct mail or email invitations to online meetings or free seminars being offered in your area. Go to a few of these to absorb the information and learn. **Keep in mind, though, that just because your local library, community center, or church "sponsors" the talk doesn't mean the presenters have been vetted.**

If you want to take things a step further, you can set up interviews with Social Security advisors online or in your area. They need to have at least one of these certifications: NSSA (National Social Security Advisor) or RSSA (Registered Social Security Analysts). They also need to have been advising people on Social Security matters for at least five years and be able to give you references. They also need to be able to discuss multiple filing options, including alternative claiming options, for your consideration. In addition, whenever you meet with them, they need to give you a checklist of information they will need from you so they can provide you with customized filing guidance and timing.

Remember what I said at the beginning of the book? **If your questions are immediately answered with an age without regard to your personal situation (finances, marriage status, family status, disability status, work status, etc.), then you should run. They should be able to outline the specific steps you need to take in order to file online or in person at the SSA, and many will even help with the online filing.** They should produce an engagement letter or online electronic agreement outlining exactly what both parties agree to as the scope of the engagement, how much it costs, and what the advisor will and won't do.

Don't forget, just because someone is an experienced Social Security "expert," that doesn't make them a Medicare insurance expert. Most everyone can outline the basic definitions of Medicare A, B, C, and D. But finding a Medicare insurance expert is usually a completely different item altogether. Not very many financial planners, wealth managers, and Social Security experts really know what they're talking about beyond the basics. You need a good book (such as *Prepare for Medicare—The Insider's Guide*), a good website (https://PrepareForMedicare.com), and a great Medicare insurance agent. These agents are typically not good Social Security experts, so don't rely on them to guide you unless you put them through the very same steps as you would above.

FINAL THOUGHTS

Now that you've learned a bit about how Social Security is marketed and the various scams out there trying to trick you, it would be easy to feel paranoid, as if everyone is out to get you. That's just not the case.

The government does what it can with limited resources to help everyone find the information they need for the benefits they are entitled to. They make mistakes, and some people fall through the cracks. But there is no reason to think the government is deliberately trying to withhold information from you.

Consultants, advisors, and private firms see a market opportunity to help people navigate the system. This is actually a useful business that can save people a lot of time and confusion and give them the peace of mind of having professionals on their side. These professionals need to be compensated for their time and expertise. Just as with any other service in a free market economy, they set their prices based on supply and demand.

Marketing techniques and market analysis tools are simply methods of researching how to reach the people who would benefit most and be most interested in what a company has to offer. It helps them be more efficient in targeting their advertising resources rather than bombarding everyone with irrelevant and irritating information.

That said, we do have to remain vigilant. Why? Because in any situation where there is a potential to make money legitimately, some people will twist it into exploitative or illegal means to take resources from people who are scared and vulnerable.

The best way not to have that happen to you is not to be scared and vulnerable. Instead, arm yourself with information, get trusted allies on your side, and refuse to be manipulated by people who try to threaten or cajole you into making a quick decision.

Speaking of trusted allies: it would be a good time to mention the specific ways I can help people. For many years, I've been asked to help people navigate Medicare, Social Security, and retirement issues in general. I genuinely love all these topics. And as I mentioned at the beginning of the book, it makes me happy to help others and educate them about these vital issues.

Why? Because they are not just theories or ideas; they have an actual impact on people's lives. If I can make a tangible, direct difference in their quality of life, and the lives of their families, I consider that time well spent.

I also enjoy being a person who connects people to experts who can help them. I like procuring experts and giving people the *Insider's Guide* to topics. I do that with my podcast, "The Matt Feret Show," as well as my books and websites. I also compile free helpful links so you don't have to spend hours searching the internet.

The podcast helps me bring you interviews with experts and insiders; I write books and create online training courses, and now I'm proud to partner with NSSA-Certified Social Security consulting services for people who want access to objective, expert Social Security consulting without a sales pitch for financial planning, insurance, or anything else. Consultants aren't free, but working with an expert isn't usually free. Whether you take advantage of my free information or paid resources (such as this book), I'm here to help.

CHAPTER SIX

UNDERSTANDING HOW SOCIAL SECURITY AND MEDICARE WORK TOGETHER

Many people are confused about the differences between Social Security and Medicare. These two separate programs work together to provide for recipients' financial and healthcare needs during their later years. The purpose of this chapter is to give a fundamental overview of how the two programs relate to each other. However, the purpose is not to offer a complete guide to Medicare.

If you'd like a fuller treatment of Medicare, please visit https://PrepareforMedicare.com and check out my book *Prepare for Medicare—The Insider's Guide.* There's a workbook available, too. I update the website and book often, so you've always got the most up-to-date information—Medicare benefits, premiums, and coverage change every year. I also invite you to sign up for my newsletter to stay up-to-date with the changes and much more!

THE DIFFERENCE BETWEEN SOCIAL SECURITY AND MEDICARE

Here's the simplest way to understand the difference between Social Security and Medicare.

Social Security pays retirement, disability, family, and survivors benefits. Benefits are based on the amount paid into Social Security payroll taxes, which are based on earnings. The higher the payments, the higher the monthly benefit (up to a limit). Social Security is meant to act as supplemental retirement insurance, not to be the primary means of support during retirement. However, many people do rely on it as their primary income. Social Security also offers benefits for people who are disabled before reaching full retirement age, as well as the beneficiary's spouse and dependents after the beneficiary dies.

On the other hand, Medicare helps pay for hospital care, nursing care, doctor visits, prescription drugs, and other medical services and supplies for people 65 and older, or those who have been on Social Security disability for two years or more.

THE RELATIONSHIP BETWEEN SOCIAL SECURITY AND MEDICARE

Social Security and Medicare are different services, but they are often confused. This is most likely because much of Medicare's administration runs through the Social Security Administration. Many of their "customers" overlap, since that includes basically every older United States citizen. The full retirement age for Social Security ranges from 66-67, depending on when you were born, but as you've already read, you can begin as early as age 62. Unless you're disabled, Medicare eligibility begins at age 65, with a three-month Initial Enrollment Period (IEP) on either side of your birth month. The IEP includes your birth month, for a total of seven.

The Social Security Administration handles enrollment for Original Medicare Parts A and B. Because of this, **if you claim your Social Security benefits before age 65, you will automatically be enrolled in Medicare when you turn 65. If you haven't applied for Social Security, you must apply for Medicare on the Social Security website or potentially face lifelong late enrollment penalties.**

A second primary connection is that the premium for Part B of Medicare will normally be deducted automatically from your monthly Social Security payment. If you are on Medicare and haven't yet elected to receive your Social Security benefits, Medicare will send you a bill. If you choose to, you may also have your Medicare Part D Prescription Drug Plan (PDP) or your Medicare Advantage Plan (MAPD) premiums withdrawn from your Social Security check. You may also have a bigger premium amount removed if you earn more money, which the SSA will decide based on the information it receives from the IRS. This is due to IRMAA, which stands for Income-Related Medicare Adjustment Amount. It's basically means-testing for Medicare premiums, and if you make more than around $91,000 per year, you may be charged an additional premium for your Medicare Part B and Medicare Part D benefits. You won't be charged a monthly premium for Medicare Part A, provided that you worked and paid Medicare taxes. For more on Medicare premiums and IRMAA, be sure to visit the Prepare for Medicare website at https://PrepareforMedicare.com and search the blog for IRMAA.

Another aspect to consider is that Social Security provides an annual cost of living increase to keep pace with increases in the Consumer Price Index. This increase may be mostly eaten up by increases in annual Medicare premiums, however. By law, Medicare premiums must be set at a level that covers 25% of the program's estimated annual cost. Some years there is no increase, but in other years there may be a substantial increase.

Because Medicare Part B premiums are usually deducted directly from Social Security checks, recipients may see little to no increase in their checks even in years where there has been a cost-of-living adjustment. Fortunately, the government has a "hold harmless rule" that does not permit increases in Medicare premiums to lower their monthly Social Security check. It's important to note, though, that the hold harmless rule does not apply to recipients who pay their premiums directly, only those who have them deducted from their Social Security checks.

ONE CHANCE TO GET IT RIGHT

One difference between Social Security and Medicare is that with Social Security, you only have one chance to get it right.

What do I mean? Once you've filed for Social Security, changing your mind can be a complicated process. You only have 12 months after you become entitled to benefits to do this, using a process called a withdrawal. You can make only one withdrawal decision in a lifetime.

This means you can choose to return the benefits you've received and go back to work if you change your mind about filing early, but you can do this only once. If you cannot withdraw, either because it has been more than 12 months or you've already used your withdrawal, and you're over full retirement age but aren't yet 70, you can suspend payments until you're 70, when they automatically kick in again.

If you withdraw, you must pay back all the money you received as benefits, including money withheld for Medicare, voluntary tax withholding, or garnishments.

Medicare, however, allows you to keep making different decisions throughout your time on the plan. If you do not apply for Original Medicare Parts A and B or Medicare Part D within the right time frame, you may pay steep lifetime fees for missing deadlines.

After you have signed up for Medicare, you can join, switch, or drop your Medicare Part D Prescription Drug Plan (PDP) or your Medicare Advantage plan annually during the Annual Election Period (AEP). Sometimes incorrectly (even by Medicare!) referred to as the Open Enrollment Period, it runs from October 15 to December 7. There's a more restrictive Medicare Advantage Open Enrollment Period (MA-OEP) from January 1 to March 31.

So, unlike Social Security, in which you decide once for the rest of your life, Medicare allows you to adjust your plan yearly as you need to unless you have a Medicare Supplement plan. Medicare Supplement plans are also called Medigap plans. Those rules are largely state-specific and too numerous to list here. For more, visit Matt's Corner Blog at https://PrepareforMedicare.com/blog and search for Medicare Supplements or Medigap in the search bar.

WHO QUALIFIES FOR MEDICARE?

To receive Medicare, you must be a U.S. citizen or permanent resident. You become eligible at age 65 or earlier if you are disabled and have been eligible for Social Security benefits for at least two years. If you have chronic kidney disease and need a transplant or dialysis, you qualify for Medicare if you have six work credits within the past three years.

To qualify for Medicare Part A, you must be eligible for Social Security retirement, disability, family or survivor payments, a pension from the Railroad Retirement Board, or you or your spouse worked for the government long enough and paid Medicare taxes.

Medicare Part B is technically optional, but I highly recommend you accept it, as not doing so leaves you ineligible for other types of Medicare insurance coverage and benefits. If you choose to accept it, you must pay a monthly premium unless you meet strict low-income guidelines. Anyone eligible for Part A may purchase Part B. It is a good decision for many people, as your monthly premium is only about 25% of the program's cost. The federal government pays the other 75% from general tax revenue, not Social Security or Medicare taxes.

Some low-income individuals and families qualify for programs to cover Part A and Part B Medicare. Some of these programs pay not only premiums but also deductibles, copays, and coinsurance. Contact your local public assistance office for more information if you think you or someone you know may qualify. You can look for links to resources at https://PrepareforMedicare.com/links.

WHAT ARE YOUR MEDICARE OPTIONS?

Medicare consists of four different programs, or "parts." Parts A and B are considered "Original Medicare." Most people 65 and older are on Medicare Parts A and B. Parts C and D allow you to purchase private insurance that supplements or combines Original Medicare Parts A and B under one plan, known as Medicare Advantage.

Let's do a quick rundown of the four parts:

Part A – Hospital insurance. This helps with the costs of inpatient hospital care, skilled nursing facility care, hospice care, and home healthcare.

Part B – Medical insurance. This helps cover services from doctors and other healthcare providers, outpatient care, home healthcare, and durable medical equipment such as wheelchairs, walkers, hospital beds, and more. It also provides preventative services such as screenings, vaccines, and annual wellness visits.

Part C – Private Medicare insurance companies sell Part C (also called Medicare Advantage, or Medicare Advantage-Prescription Drug plans (MAPD). These are plans that combine Medicare Parts A, B, and D and may offer additional benefits such as vision, hearing, or dental services not covered by Original Medicare.

Part D – Prescription drug coverage plans. Private Medicare insurance companies provide stand-alone Medicare Part D Prescription Drug Plans (PDP). They cover some of the costs of prescription drugs, shots, and vaccinations. Some Part D benefits are embedded within Medicare Advantage plans (MAPD), but Part D generally refers to the stand-alone Prescription Drug Plan you match to Original Medicare A and B or without a Medicare Supplement plan. More on this below.

Note that individual states sometimes have additional Medicare Supplemental or Medigap options.

There are two steps for Medicare. First, you sign up for or simply accept Part A (hospital insurance) and Part B (medical insurance). Generally, you only need to do that once, and you choose how you receive that coverage each year, choosing Part C, Part D, or others, depending on the coverage you desire.

HOW DO YOU ENROLL IN MEDICARE?

Some people are automatically enrolled in Medicare, but not everyone. If you are already getting retirement payments from Social Security or the Railroad Retirement Board, you will be auto-enrolled in Original Medicare Parts A and B the first month you reach 65. If you're drawing Social Security before age 65 because of a disability, you will be auto-enrolled after 24 months of disability payments. If you don't want to be enrolled in Medicare Part B under any of these circumstances, you can drop it and keep Medicare Part A, which doesn't have a monthly premium for all but a very small percentage of people. Just follow the instructions you receive in the mail with your red, white, and blue Original Medicare card.

If, at age 65, you are not yet drawing Social Security or a railroad pension, you will not be auto-enrolled. If you or your spouse have employee health coverage from your job(s), and don't want to enroll in Medicare at 65, you may enroll close to your retirement date or when your employer's healthcare plan ends.

If you neglect to file for Medicare at 65, you may still enroll at a later date, but lifelong late fees may be added to your Medicare Part B and Medicare Part D premiums. When you enroll, your coverage begins on the first day of the month after filing. For example, if you enroll in January, your Medicare Part B coverage begins on February 1. If you delay enrolling in Medicare Part B past age 65 and don't have another type of qualifying health insurance, such as an employer-sponsored or ACA health insurance plan, your monthly premiums are permanently increased by 10% for each year you wait past your birthday. For each month you delay enrollment in Medicare Part D, you will have to pay a 1% Part D late enrollment penalty.

As I've previously noted, Medicare is such a nuanced and difficult topic in its own right, I've written an entire book on the subject! If you'd like to know more, visit the book's website at https://PrepareforMedicare.com.

WHAT ARE THE IMPLICATIONS OF FILING FOR MEDICARE BEFORE FILING FOR SOCIAL SECURITY?

Most people become eligible to file for Medicare at age 65. If you are already drawing Social Security at that age, the Social Security Administration will automatically enroll you in Medicare.

Because so many people start drawing Social Security on or before age 65, it's a common misconception that you must apply for Social Security and Medicare simultaneously. Even Social Security Administration employees and online calculators sometimes seem to assume this. Often, when asked for estimates of benefits, they quote a figure with Medicare Part B premium payments deducted since these are taken out of your monthly Social Security check.

However, if you don't wish to draw Social Security on or before age 65, you don't have to. You can still start Medicare alone at 65. However, in this situation, the SSA will not automatically enroll you. You'll have to go to the SSA.gov website to enroll yourself in Medicare. Your Part B premiums will be billed directly to you.

Suppose you do start Medicare at age 65 but decide to delay drawing your Social Security benefits until later. In that case, you must proactively sign up for Medicare on SSA.gov and pay your Part B premiums directly to Medicare.

THREE WAYS TO "CONSUME" YOUR MEDICARE BENEFITS

The information in this section is explained in more detail in my book *Prepare for Medicare—The Insider's Guide,* but I will provide you with a concise summary here. There are generally three ways you can use your Medicare benefits, summarized in the chart below:

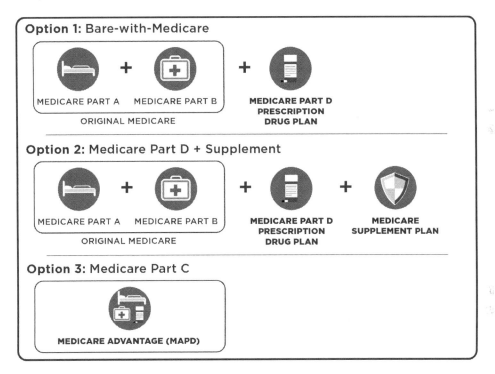

OPTION 1: BARE-WITH-MEDICARE

In this option, you use Original Medicare parts A and B for your medical insurance coverage and buy a Medicare Part D Prescription Drug Plan to cover your prescription drug insurance.

This is the easiest way to consume your Medicare benefits. One advantage of this approach is that you don't have any network restrictions to deal with. It has lower premiums than option #2 below.

On the downside, there is no annual medical maximum out-of-pocket cost limit, also called a MOOP. As a result, your financial exposure could be unlimited. You will pay 20% coinsurance for medical care, and you may face Medicare excess charges. Coverage for overseas travel is limited. It doesn't include the extra coverages that Medicare Advantage plans offer, and deductibles and premiums usually go up every year.

OPTION 2: MEDICARE PART D + SUPPLEMENT

This option involves the same coverage as Option 1: Medicare Part A, B, and D, but also purchasing a Medicare Supplement plan to cover you for the portion of medical costs Original Medicare doesn't cover. Medicare Supplement plans are also called Medigap plans.

Something that makes this approach a bit simpler is that most Medicare insurance companies offering Medicare Supplement coverage sell plans with identical benefits that follow a letter coding system. This makes it much easier to shop around for the best price and know that you are comparing apples to apples, not sacrificing coverage for a lower price. Be forewarned, though; some states have different Medicare Supplement rules and plans than others.

Other advantages of Medicare Supplement plans are that they have guaranteed renewability. As long as you pay your premiums, you cannot be kicked off the plan. Benefits do not change every year. There are no networks or provider network hoops to jump through, and no referrals are required. Some plans provide limited coverage for overseas travel. These plans work cooperatively with Original Medicare to cover the uncovered portion of your medical bills without you having to get involved or file separate claims.

A disadvantage of this option is that you will have to buy two insurance policies (a Medicare Part D Prescription Drug Plan (PDP) and a separate Medicare Supplement) and pay premiums on two separate insurance policies. Premiums for Medicare Supplement plans are not cheap, costing as much as $150-200+ a month, and premiums generally increase as you get older.

It's also important to know that if you sign up for a Medicare Supplement plan during the open enrollment period (within the first six months of getting

Medicare Part B), the company must accept you regardless of your health status. If you miss this window, you may have to answer health questions and could be denied coverage based on your answers. In some cases, these policies do not pay to treat preexisting conditions for the first six months of your coverage. There can also be difficulties switching back and forth between Medicare Advantage and Medicare Supplements that may result in your losing coverage.

OPTION 3: MEDICARE PART C—MEDICARE ADVANTAGE

Finally, you have the option of buying a Medicare Advantage plan (MAPD) that covers your medical costs as well as your prescription drug costs, with no need to purchase a stand-alone Medicare Part D Prescription Drug Plan (PDP). These plans cover the medical benefits of Original Medicare Parts A, B, and D in what could be considered a "combo" plan.

These plans can be very affordable, with premiums anywhere from $0-100 a month. There are copays for doctor visits, deductibles, and coinsurance, and all of them must have a maximum out-of-pocket expense limit. Many services do not have deductibles or coinsurance unless you use an out-of-network provider or need certain categories of prescription drugs.

Moreover, many of these plans offer benefits such as dental, vision, and hearing coverage. These are just a few of many things not covered by Original Medicare Part A or Part B. Only Medicare Advantage plans have care management programs for people with chronic conditions such as high blood pressure, diabetes, heart failure, end-stage renal disease, rheumatoid arthritis, depression, and others. If you sign up during the correct time frame, you can never be denied coverage, as medical underwriting for these products is prohibited.

Once again, no plan is perfect. Here are some of the disadvantages of Option 3: The benefits in a Medicare Advantage plan can (and do!) change every year. Monthly premiums may fluctuate year by year, and while the monthly premiums may be lower than those of a Medicare Supplement, the coverage may not be as comprehensive. A $0 premium plan may increase to $40 the next year. Depending on where you live, there may be a lack of plan choices, or so many choices that it is overwhelming. Although you cannot be dropped from coverage if you're paying your premiums on time, your plan could be canceled, forcing you to choose a different one. If you purchase an HMO plan, it typically requires referrals.

One of the biggest disadvantages is the necessity to work with providers who are in-network, which can be distressing if your longstanding family physician or favorite pharmacy is not in-network. If you choose to work with professionals outside the network, you could face all charges that exceed what is permitted by the network. At the very least, they'll be paid at an "out-of-network" status. Provider directories are often outdated or wrong, so you need to call the provider directly to verify they accept your plan before scheduling an appointment. It also happens from time to time that a doctor leaves or the insurance company cancels your doctor's or hospital's contract in the middle of a year, leaving you with a choice between finding a new provider or sticking with your current one and paying any excess charges.

COMPLEX, BUT WORTH THE TROUBLE

No doubt, in many ways, Medicare is even more complicated than Social Security. But it is an important program keeping healthcare affordable for millions of retired Americans. Without it, many people would experience a lower quality of life, endure needless suffering, and have a shorter lifespan.

For all these reasons, it's worth your while to do the work to understand the program and seek out trusted and knowledgeable people who can help you make the best decisions for your situation. And as always, you can visit https://PrepareforMedicare.com to sign up for my newsletter, read Matt's Corner Blog, and purchase my books and courses.

CHAPTER SEVEN

FILING FOR SOCIAL SECURITY BENEFITS: DIY (DO-IT-YOURSELF)

I've mentioned in previous chapters that you might want to call on a specialist to help you with various aspects of Social Security and Medicare. Remember, you only get one chance to get this right!

It can take a good deal of networking, interviewing, and assessing the right trained, licensed, certified, experienced, and trustworthy consultant, Medicare insurance agent, or financial planner. However, they can help you figure out when to file and what benefits to file for so you can create the best financial situation for yourself and your family. If you're interested in fee-only Social Security consulting, I offer access to NSSA-certified professionals through the website at https://PrepareforSocialSecurity.com.

All that said, you can absolutely go through the filing process independently. In this chapter, I'll take you step-by-step through the basics of a do-it-yourself approach to filing. The first place to begin is by using one of the most basic, yet important tools the SSA makes available: benefits calculators. All information found in this chapter was current at the time of publication, but be sure to check out the Prepare for Social Security website for the most up-to-date information.

USING BENEFITS CALCULATORS TO HELP YOU MAKE A DECISION

Benefits calculators can be incredibly helpful in giving you information to make good decisions related to Social Security. However, **it is generally best not to rely on only one benefits calculator when deciding when to retire and start claiming benefits.** Even excellent tools can have occasional bugs. Also, keep in mind that your benefits will increase with inflation. (You can find links to all the resources mentioned here by visiting https://PrepareforSocialSecurity.com/links.)

One excellent calculator is the Retirement Estimator from the SSA itself. This calculator uses your actual earnings record through your "*my Social Security*" account to give your estimate. This tool does not recommend the best age to start benefits, but it does show your estimated benefits if you start payments at age 62, full retirement age, and age 70. Additionally, you can only use this tool if you have enough Social Security credits (40 credits).

If you don't have and don't want to have a "*my Social Security*" account yet, you can use the "Online Benefits Calculator" from the SSA. However, you must put in all your earnings information every time you use it to get an accurate estimate. Because of this, they recommend using the "*my Social Security*" account since it is easier and faster.

The fastest SSA calculator is the Quick Calculator. Keep in mind that it uses very little data and, as such, is not necessarily accurate. It "makes an initial assumption about your past earnings," which you can change to make it more accurate.

The SSA also provides a Retirement Age Calculator, which shows your full retirement age based on your year of birth, and an Early or Late Retirement Calculator. This one will show the estimated impact on your benefits if you retire earlier or later than your full retirement age.

All SSA calculators are available on their "Benefits Calculators" page. If you plan to have additional income during retirement, the Retirement Earnings Test Calculator from the SSA can estimate how much of your benefit might be withheld in taxes.

You can also use any number of third-party retirement calculators, which again only provide estimates. You can find a list of these in our Links sections at https://PrepareforSocialSecurity.com/links.

FILING YOUR APPLICATION

There are three ways to complete the application. The easiest is to apply online, though you can also choose to phone or go to a Social Security office. You can find all SSA office locations, Google Map driving directions, and phone numbers on the Prepare for Social Security website, too.

APPLYING ONLINE

- To start your application, go to the Social Security Administration website, navigate to the "Apply for Benefits" page, and read and agree to the Terms of Service. Click "Next."

- Review the "Getting Ready" section on the next page to ensure you have the information you need to apply.

- Select "Start A New Application."

- Answer the questions about who is filling out the application.

- You will be prompted to sign in to your Social Security account or to create one.

- Complete the application.

The SSA provides a few tips for completing this application. First, they note that for security reasons, it is best not to leave the application open without doing anything for more than 25 minutes. Additionally, if you get stuck on a question, you can move on to a different question and return at a later point. You can save your application and finish it later if you need. You can also access saved applications by going to "Return to a Saved Application" after you sign in. Finally, some answers (such as addresses) do not allow using periods, commas, or other special characters. If you get a message that your answer isn't valid, check this first since it is likely the culprit.

Once you have completed the application, it will give you a chance to confirm your answers and make any necessary changes. It will ask if the answers are true to the best of your knowledge and inform you that you can be held liable if you have provided false or misleading information in your application. After you have reviewed your information, you can click "submit now" to digitally sign your application. It will then provide a confirmation number which you can use to check the status of your application.

If you want to complete your application at the local Social Security office, check your local office's address on the Prepare for Social Security webpage at https://PrepareforSocialSecurity.com or at https://secure.ssa.gov/ICON/main.jsp by putting in your ZIP Code. You can also call 1-800-772-1213 from 8:00 a.m. to 7:00 p.m. Monday through Friday to apply by phone.

WHAT RECORDS SHOULD YOU KEEP?

To be ready for the application, you will need the following information and documents at the ready (source: https://PrepareforSocialSecurity.com/sources):

- ✓ Your birth date, place of birth, and Social Security number.

- ✓ The name, Social Security number, and date of birth or age of your spouse(s), current or former. You should also know the dates and places of marriage and dates of divorce or death (if applicable).

- ✓ The names of any unmarried children under age 18, age 18-19 and in elementary or secondary school, or disabled before age 22.

- ✓ Your bank or other financial institution's Routing Transit Number and the account number.

- ✓ Your citizenship status.

- Whether you or anyone else has ever filed for Social Security benefits, Medicare, or Supplemental Security Income on your behalf.

- Whether you have used any other Social Security number.

- If you are applying for retirement benefits, the month you want your benefits to begin; and

- If you are within three months of age 65, whether you want to enroll in Medical Insurance (Part B of Medicare).

- The name and address of your employer(s) for the current and previous year.

- How much money you earned in the current and previous years. If you are filing for benefits from September through December, you will also need to estimate your anticipated earnings for the next year.

- A copy of your Social Security Statement or your earnings record. If you do not have a Statement, you can view your Social Security Statement online by creating an account and signing in. Even if you do not have a record of your earnings or are unsure if they are correct, you should fill out your application, and the SSA will help you review your earnings.

- The beginning and end dates of any active U.S. military service you had before 1968.

- Whether you became unable to work because of illnesses, injuries, or conditions at any time within the past 14 months. If "Yes," they will also ask the date you became unable to work.

- Whether you or your spouse have ever worked for the railroad industry.

- Whether you have earned Social Security credits under another country's Social Security system; and

- Whether you qualified for or expect to receive a pension or annuity based on your own employment with the federal government of the United States or one of its states or local subdivisions.

Additional documents you may need:

- Your original birth certificate or other proof of birth.
- Proof of U.S. citizenship or lawful alien status if you were not born in the United States.
- A copy of your U.S. military service paper(s) (e.g., DD-214 Certificate of Release or Discharge from Active Duty) and
- A copy of your W-2 form(s) and/or self-employment tax return for last year.

The SSA will accept copies of W-2 forms, self-employment tax returns, or medical documents but must see the original of most other documents, including your birth certificate. These will be returned to you.

When mailing documents to the SSA, be sure to include your Social Security number on a separate sheet of paper so that they will be matched to the correct file. If you have foreign birth records or documents from the Department of Homeland Security, do not mail them because they are extremely difficult to replace. Instead, bring them to your local Social Security office for examination.

You should keep careful records so you can confirm your income from every year you worked, preferably with tax information as well. This ensures you are getting your proper benefit amount. That way, you can double-check the benefit amount by logging into your account and confirming that it's correct.

TAX IMPLICATIONS OF FILING FOR SOCIAL SECURITY

Tax on Social Security benefits is complicated. Some people will have to pay income tax on their benefits, and others won't. It's based entirely on your income and where you live in retirement. The SSA claims that you will likely only have to pay tax on your benefits if you have other income from wages, self-employment, interest, dividends, or other taxable income.

Here are the SSA and IRS rules for paying federal income tax on your Social Security benefits. If you:

- **File a federal tax return as an "individual,"** and your combined income is
    - between $25,000 and $34,000—you may have to pay income tax on up to 50% of your benefits.
    - more than $34,000—up to 85% of your benefits may be taxable.
- **File a joint return,** and you and your spouse have a combined income that is
    - between $32,000 and $44,000—you may have to pay income tax on up to 50% of your benefits.
    - more than $44,000—up to 85% of your benefits may be taxable.
- **Are married and file a separate tax return,** you will probably pay taxes on your benefits.

The amounts above are set and have not changed since the law was first passed to tax Social Security benefits in 1983, then amended in 1993. This was purposely done to benefit lower-income people, with the understanding that because the levels were not indexed to inflation, they should become less burdensome over time (source: https://PrepareforSocialSecurity.com).

Also note that the SSA defines a combined income as your adjusted gross income, plus nontaxable interest, plus half of your Social Security benefits.

If you have to pay federal taxes on your benefits, you get to choose if you want them automatically withheld from your benefits or if you want to make estimated tax payments to the IRS four times a year.

HOW DO YOU DETERMINE YOUR SOCIAL SECURITY BENEFIT AMOUNT?

One way to get a quick idea is to look at the average numbers. The average retired worker currently receives over $1,500 per month, or nearly $20,000 per year. However, looking at just the straight averages are deceiving, since Social Security benefits are progressive. If you earned less during your time working, your benefits would be a higher percentage of your former earnings. If you earned more, your benefits would be a higher dollar amount than if you earned less, but a lower percentage of your previous earnings.

Here is a chart, for example, based on data from a table called "Annual Scheduled Benefit Amounts for Retired Workers With Various Pre-Retirement Earnings Patterns Based on Intermediate Assumptions" from the SSA. Low earnings are 45% of the career-average earnings, medium earnings are 100%, and high earnings are 160%. The maximum earnings are earnings for each year that are at or above the contribution and benefit base, which works out to about 240%. This chart is inspired by but based on the newest data from the SSA.

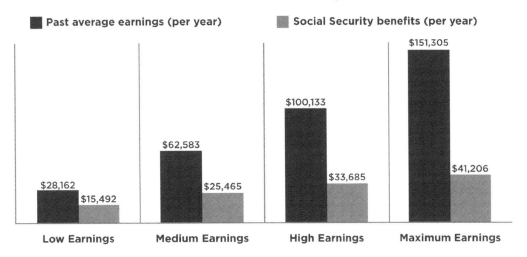

Chart based on information from https://www.ssa.gov/oact/TR/2022/lr5c7.html

An even better way to determine your Social Security benefit amount is to use an online calculator. We talked about several of these earlier in the chapter, but it may be helpful here to summarize how to use two in particular to determine your benefit amount.

The SSA offers what they call a "Quick Calculator," where you can enter your date of birth, your current year's earnings, and the month and year you are hoping to retire. Note that this calculator does not take your past earnings into account. You can find similar calculators on numerous other websites.

However, the SSA offers what many argue is the most accurate calculator through your "*my Social Security*" account. This calculator will take your earnings history and give a solid estimate of your potential benefits. Again, **note that your Medicare premium and taxes could potentially be taken out of these benefits, so don't take them totally at face value.** (For links to all calculators mentioned here, please visit our Links page at https://PrepareforSocialSecurity.com/links.)

THE APPEALS PROCESS FOR SOCIAL SECURITY ADMINISTRATION DECISIONS

Many of the decisions made by the SSA can be appealed if you disagree with them. In their language, the initial decisions they make are called "initial determinations." These constitute the SSA's findings on legal issues, the amount of your benefit payment, and issues related to overpayments, and they can be appealed.

Whenever the SSA makes an initial determination, they will send you a notice. Then you have 60 days to appeal that determination in writing. The notice will tell you both how to appeal and whether you are entitled to continued benefits while you appeal.

Be forewarned that when you appeal an SSA decision, they will reexamine your entire case, even those parts that were favorable to you. **This means there is a chance that some of your benefits may be reduced through the appeals process if they realize they made a mistake that turned out to be favorable to you.**

There are four levels, or steps, in the appeals process. Each level has a 60-day window, plus five days the SSA allows for mail delivery. (Visit https://PrepareforSocialSecurity.com/links for links to SSA pages that go into more detail about each of these levels.)

The first is "Reconsideration." If you don't agree with the SSA's initial determination, you may request reconsideration. The quickest way to do this is to go to the "Appeal a Decision" page and choose the right reconsideration, whether medical or non-medical. You can also submit a form by mail or fax. This will be "a complete review of your claim by someone who did not take part in the first determination. They will look at all the evidence used in the first determination, plus any new evidence that we obtain or that you submit."

The second level of appeal, if you don't agree with the reconsideration determination, is a "Hearing by Administrative Law Judge." There is an online request for you to fill out where you will select whether it is medical or non-medical. While you may ask the judge to make a decision based on the evidence in your file, you are much more likely to be successful if you or your representative appear before the judge for the hearing. You can request that your hearing take place in person, by video teleconference, or by telephone, but the SSA will determine the manner of your court appearance in the end. The judge may ask medical and vocational experts to testify at the hearing.

The third level of appeal, if you don't agree with the judge's decision, is an Appeals Council review. You can submit a written appeal or fill out an online form. Like the others, this must be submitted within 60 days after the previous decision. You can submit or inform the council about new evidence. The Appeals Council will consider an appeal based on additional evidence if it is new and relevant, and it is reasonable to think it would affect the final decision. From there, they decide whether or not to grant your request for review. They may deny or dismiss the request if they conclude the decision conforms to Social Security law and regulations. They may also decide to issue a new decision or send it to an administrative law judge for a decision.

Finally, the fourth and final level of appeal, if all else fails, is the Federal Court review. If you disagree with the action of the Appeals Council, you may file a civil action in the U.S. District Court in your area. Note that the SSA will not help you file this, and you will not be able to file online. You will likely need a lawyer or other legal counsel to take this step.

NAVIGATING THE BUREAUCRACY

As with any large organization, the SSA has many layers of people and processes to go through in order to get nearly anything done. As you read in the previous section, there can be many steps to processes such as appealing a decision. On the plus side, many things in the SSA are not as complicated, especially with online capabilities. To that end, this section is meant to help you understand and navigate the vast amount of information from this large organization.

The highest level in the SSA is the Commissioner, who oversees, supports, and advises all other functions in the SSA. Then, there are a number of Deputy Commissioners, each in charge of different departments, which are in turn divided into even smaller departments focused on various things.

Depending on your needs, you will be impacted by or interact with many of these departments.

There are Deputy Commissioners of:

- Analytics, Review, and Oversight – Reviews effectiveness, makes data-based recommendations for improvement, detects and prevents fraud, and works with external monitoring authorities.

- Budget, Finance, and Management – Takes care of the budget, acquisitions, grants, facilities, logistics, security, and emergency preparedness. They also develop agency policies and procedures and manage the financial systems.

- Communications – Works with national organizations, advocacy groups, other federal agencies, state and local governments, and the White House while also educating and working with the public.

- Hearings Operations – Facilitates individual or organization appeals of determinations made by the SSA. As such, this department includes many Administrative Law Judges across the nation.

- Human Resources – Manages personnel, management, and employee relations and training.

- Legislation and Congressional Affairs – Works with Congress and the Executive Branch on SSA legislation.

- Operations – Coordinates and implements the electronic systems for delivering SSA services to the public, studying needs in various regions of the country (including their call answering and service centers).

- Retirement/Disability Policy – Advises the Commissioner on policy issues, strategic planning, research, analysis, and implementation of policies.

- Systems – Oversees software and hardware procedures, policies, and activities throughout the development, validation, and implementation phases.

The SSA also includes the offices of:

- Chief Actuary – Evaluates and analyzes the Federal Old Age and Survivors Insurance Trust Fund and the Federal Disability Trust Fund, estimating and predicting what will happen in the future.

- Civil Rights and Equal Opportunity – Manages the SSA programs related to civil rights, equal opportunity, diversity, and inclusion, harassment prevention, reasonable accommodations, and disability services.

- General Counsel – Advises the SSA Commissioner and Deputy Commissioners on legal matters, as well as developing and implementing privacy and disclosure policies.

THE SOCIAL SECURITY WEBSITE

The front page of their website is fairly easy to navigate. You can see online services, retirement services, disability services, SSI, and Medicare information without scrolling. There are also buttons for "How to Get Help" and "FAQs." You can also click the "Search" icon at the top of the page and look for your question, which often leads you to the right place. As you scroll down, there is a number of items of interest, including calculators, publications, forms, and their "Contact Us" page.

This contact page is quite comprehensive. They give options for calling, writing, emailing, or locating a local office. Additionally, they provide free interpretation services if you don't speak English and have capabilities to serve you if you are blind or visually impaired, deaf or hard of hearing, or live in a different part of the world. If you are in any number of smaller groups, the SSA also has a "People Like Me" page that can help you find information tailored to you. (See https://PrepareforSocialSecurity.com/links for links to the pages mentioned in this section.)

APPOINTING A REPRESENTATIVE

One very important part of navigating the bureaucracy is knowing that you can appoint a representative to assist you if necessary. They can help you:

- ✓ Collect information
- ✓ File forms
- ✓ Understand how the law applies to your file
- ✓ Collect and review notices and letters on your behalf
- ✓ Represent you at hearings
- ✓ Understand and file appeals

There is a process to appoint the representative, including signing a statement naming them your representative. While your representative doesn't have to be a lawyer, they do need to meet specific requirements. If they are an attorney, they must be licensed and should have good character and skills. They must not have been disqualified, suspended, or legally prohibited from representing people before the SSA.

FILING SURVIVORS BENEFITS CLAIMS

Survivors benefits are paid to widows, widowers, and dependents of eligible workers. If you are a worker who pays into Social Security, a portion of those taxes covers survivors benefits. In effect, this is a form of life insurance that can be worth hundreds of thousands of dollars to you.

You should notify SSA as soon as possible if someone dies. To do this, you must call them, as there is not an online system to report a death or apply for survivors benefits. Instead, you should call them at 1-800-772-1213 or contact your local office.

There is a one-time death payment of $255 when someone dies, paid to either the surviving spouse or the child eligible for benefits. You must then repay any Social Security benefits the deceased may have received during the month of their death and any subsequent months. There are many requirements and slight differences in how much you may receive or if you are eligible for survivors benefits based on varying circumstances, ages, and other factors.

In general, if you are not already receiving Social Security benefits, you should apply right away for survivors benefits because the benefits may not be retroactive. If you are receiving benefits based on your spouse's or parent's work record, you will not typically need to file an application, as the changes should happen automatically. However, it is still good to make sure the SSA knows about the death. If you are receiving benefits based on your own work record, you will need to apply for survivors benefits.

To apply, you will need different documents depending on what benefits you are applying for. These can include proof of the worker's death, proof of your birth, proof of citizenship, tax returns, and marriage or divorce certificates. These are the various forms showing what you may need for different benefits (you can find links to all these forms at https://PrepareforSocialSecurity.com/links).

- Widows/Widowers or Surviving Divorced Spouse's Benefits
- Child's Benefits
- Mother's or Father's Benefits
- Lump-Sum Death Payment
- Parent's Benefits (if you're dependent on your child at the time of his or her death)

FEELING OVERWHELMED?

I've thrown a lot of information at you, but just take it step by step, and you'll get there. Remember that all the different options of calculators are just tools to help you estimate your benefit amounts. They're not there to frustrate you. Don't feel you have to try every one.

My recommendation is to use the SSA calculator and compare it with two or three others. If you get roughly the same results for each, it's a good bet that it's close to what you'll be getting. If you have wildly differing numbers, look more closely at exactly what each calculator is measuring.

In the end, what matters is what the SSA decides your benefit amount will be and whether you wish to dispute their findings to try to get more. You must determine whether the disputed amount is significant enough to justify the appeals process's time, energy, and expense. However, if there is a large amount of money at stake and you have a good case, then, by all means, use the appeals process—that's exactly what it's there for.

CHAPTER EIGHT

FILING FOR SOCIAL SECURITY BENEFITS: HIRE A CONSULTANT OR ADVISOR

This chapter will help you decide whether or not you want to hire a professional consultant or advisor to help you work through the intricacies of the Social Security system. We'll look at how to determine if such a person is a legitimate professional, the different types of professionals available, how to prepare for a meeting with them, and how they typically get paid. A good consultant or advisor can make all the difference in the world. If you already know you would benefit from going this route, visit https://PrepareforSocialSecurity.com for NSSA-certified, fee-only Social Security consulting.

SHOULD YOU HIRE A CONSULTANT?

The primary reasons for deciding if you should hire a consultant are whether or not you feel comfortable with your ability to navigate the Social Security Administration, if you're married, plan to continue working, or have other special tax and financial planning considerations. An enormous number of online resources and books is available to help you (such as the one you're reading!).

It's also not hard to find someone who has recently retired or helped a loved one through the process who might be able to guide you thanks to their experience. The SSA personnel themselves are available to answer your questions by phone or in person at an SSA office. **Remember though, that SSA employees are not supposed to provide advice, although sometimes they may attempt to.** In the end, you are the only one who can make the best decisions for your situation and family.

Nevertheless, it can be confusing and stressful, especially because your decisions have long-term ramifications and can rarely if ever, be reversed. Some people appreciate the peace of mind of knowing someone who specializes in this field who can help them make the best decisions.

Throughout our lives, we hire doctors, attorneys, computer specialists, mechanics, and other professionals to provide services and advice we are not skilled enough to provide for ourselves. Getting help with Social Security planning is no different. Even highly skilled financial advisors often consult other professionals in difficult situations or for help with their own retirement planning. It isn't easy to separate emotion from our decisions when handling our money. An outside professional can look at our situation objectively and give us logical advice.

Here are a few practical reasons why many people decide that hiring a consultant is a good investment. They can help you:

- Understand the process clearly and simply.
- Investigate solutions for your unique situation.
- Understand the tax implications of your decision.
- Plan for medical and retirement expenses in ways you hadn't considered.
- Navigate through the appeals process if you need to use it.
- Be aware of additional benefits you may have overlooked.

Without an advisor, you are on your own to make decisions about Social Security. You can use the calculators and free tools on the SSA website and other places. Still, ultimately you make the final decisions, which may or may not match up with what you calculated using online resources. Advisors and consultants often have extra software and programs to confirm your choices, which automatically run many of the numbers you must input manually with the SSA website.

A short caveat: while a consultant or advisor can be a great asset, there are two instances when you may need to get help from an attorney. The first is if you need to appeal a determination. With the various steps and bureaucracy of that process and the levels of judges and courts, it is good to hire an attorney with experience dealing with these sorts of claims. The second is when you are filing for Social Security disability.

What are the downsides of seeking professional help? Only a few, but they are significant:

- They may be more skilled in some areas than others (disability vs. retirement) but not always in the areas you require.
- They may offer consulting services but not have the appropriate experience or industry-standard qualifications.
- They may give away "free" or low-cost Social Security advice or consulting as a way to push financial planning services at a later date.

All this underscores the importance of doing your homework to find a reputable, honest professional rather than picking the first name you find online or see in an advertisement.

HOW CAN YOU KNOW WHETHER SOMEONE IS A LEGITIMATE PROFESSIONAL?

One way to find a consultant is to ask for recommendations from people you know and trust. If your friend or acquaintance worked with this individual on a similar issue and had a genuinely good experience, their advice may be helpful. Some people, though, make second- or third-hand recommendations from a friend of a friend or based on seeing an advertisement themselves. Those kinds of recommendations are often no better than your intuition.

Another way to find a consultant is to search on the internet. Be forewarned; you'll likely have to research and vet several Social Security "experts" if you go this route. You'll be able to put together your own list of potential contacts from which you can choose.

Before committing to a Social Security advisor or consultant, it's a great idea to interview the expert you're thinking of hiring. Here are some focuses for your questions that will help you notice any red flags:

- Ask basic questions about the company's history, philosophy, and services and how long they have been in business. Do their answers match the impression you formed of them from their website?
- Ask about their education. What are their credentials, certifications, or affiliations that corroborate their claim to be able to provide financial advice?
- Does what they say about the basics of Social Security benefits line up with what you've learned in this book and other sources? If what they say is radically different, buyer beware!
- Ask what software they use for retirement planning. If they say they don't, or only use the "free" ones found online, move on!
- Request references from other financial professionals.

When meeting with a consultant or advisor, notice whether they are patient with your questions. If they are impatient or short with you on the phone, immediately thank them for their time and go on to the next name on your list. If they are impatient with you at this stage, they are not in the right business.

Take note, even if someone has been in their profession for a long time, this may not mean they are thoroughly qualified. Here's an example based on a real firm, with the names changed to respect privacy:

"Wilson V. Ball & Associates" builds a good case for their services on their website and on LinkedIn. They specialize in Social Security disability, have completed thousands of cases, and have an easy-to-follow website that lists the steps you need to take and all the services they can provide for you. You don't see any red flags.

Look a little closer, though. What are Mr. Ball's qualifications? How many "associates" are there? Who are they, and what are their qualifications? One way to find out more is to consult a competitor. After reaching out to Cas T. Way, Attorney-at-Law, you'll find out that there are no attorneys at Wilson V. Ball & Associates, only consultants. This means they will not be able to represent their clients as a trained lawyer through all the different levels of appeal. Even though they did not complete law school and are unlicensed and uninsured, their fees are as high as professional lawyers.

This is just one example of the benefit of doing your research before choosing a consultant or other professional expert.

WHAT KINDS OF PROFESSIONALS CAN YOU HIRE TO HELP WITH SOCIAL SECURITY?

Below are three reputable professional associations that provide training, testing, and certification on Social Security issues. Look for these professional designations when using an advisor or consultant to help you make decisions. *Note: all advisors affiliated with Prepare for Social Security are certified by the NSSA.*

- National Association of Registered Social Security Analysts Ltd. (NARSSA)
- National Association of Personal Finance Advisors (NAPFA)
- National Social Security Association (NSSA)

Membership in these can be another reassuring indication that the person you are considering hiring has some qualifications that have been evaluated by a third party and has to maintain a good reputation to remain affiliated with those associations.

FINANCIAL PLANNERS AND WEALTH MANAGERS

FINRA, the Financial Industry Regulatory Authority (a government-authorized regulating body), lists 224 professional designations or credentials and the combinations of numbers you may see after a financial professional's name. You can find their website at https://www.finra.org/investors/professional-designations.

Note that the term "retirement advisor" is just a marketing tool, not an official designation or credential. There's nothing dishonest about the term. It's just a way to communicate to the public what service they offer. The best way to evaluate a retirement advisor is not by their title but by their skills and expertise.

Some of the more common titles you might see include:

- Certified Financial Planner (CFP) – This is a recognized expert in financial planning, taxes, insurance, estate planning, and retirement. A CFP has higher education in their field, has passed standardized exams, and has demonstrated experience and ethical integrity. They also have a fiduciary duty, which means they must make decisions with the client's best interests in mind.

- Chartered Retirement Plans Specialist (CRPS) – This professional develops and manages retirement plans for businesses. They are required to complete 16 hours of continuing education every two years to maintain their status.

- Retirement Income Certified Professional (RICP) – This is an expert in retirement income planning. To earn this designation, they must have three years of business experience and complete three courses with exams.

- Chartered Retirement Planning Counselor (CRPC) – This professional concentrates on helping clients work through retirement-related problems. They must complete six courses before receiving the CRPC designation and 16 hours of continuing education every two years.

WHAT TO EXPECT AT AN APPOINTMENT

If you're paying a Social Security professional or advisor, they will ask you a series of questions and then explain how to file for Social Security. Sometimes they will do it with you, or for you. They will not be able to help you with a comprehensive financial plan, only with questions related directly to Social Security. Since you're paying them for Social Security consulting, you should expect them to complete the service to your satisfaction and not pressure you to buy additional insurance, financial planning products, or likewise.

Each professional will have their own process for onboarding new clients. In many cases, you can buy a consulting package right on their website (just like on the Prepare for Social Security website). They may have an online form for you to complete before your appointment.

Your Social Security advisor or financial professional should tell you what to bring with you when you meet or chat. They may need documents describing your financial situation, including your earnings, your current investment and bank account holdings, and any other information that would give them an accurate picture of your finances. They will usually have you send your information before your appointment so they don't waste your time getting acquainted with your financial information during the appointment.

Make sure your advisor focuses on your retirement wants and needs. If you get the sense they are pushing advice or products that aren't a good fit for your situation, then find a different advisor. **It doesn't hurt to see more than one and compare their advice, especially if they offer the initial consultation and financial plan free of charge.** Don't feel guilty if you only use their free services and decline sales pitches for products you don't need. They wouldn't keep making these offers unless they're finding plenty of other customers who want what they're selling.

HOW DO SOCIAL SECURITY ADVISORS GET PAID?

There are two main ways Social Security advisors get paid, depending on the type of services they offer.

Professional Social Security advisors or consultants work on a fee-only basis. You pay a fee and get Social Security filing advice for retirement. However, financial planners or wealth managers may or may not charge a fee. When they offer free services, it's generally because they will try to get you into more products like financial planning services, life insurance annuities, etc.

Some financial advisors have a percentage-based fee structure that, in the case of retirement investments, may charge a lower percentage the larger your account balance. Sometimes, an advisor will charge a percentage of the award received from a successful disability claim.

Some advisors may be "free" but receive commissions when you purchase financial products from them. If you are interested in commission-based products, ask them to itemize the amount of compensation they receive from their recommended products. If they encourage you to buy something that delivers a large commission to them, you may want to investigate further to ensure it is of genuine benefit to you.

NAPFA (the National Association of Personal Financial Advisors) offers a form that a financial advisor can fill out. It will give you an exact idea of how they charge fees and commissions. You can find websites that will point you to reputable, fee-only firms.

(You can find links for all of the above at https://PrepareforSocialSecurity.com/links.)

THE BOTTOM LINE

Hiring a professional consultant to help you with your Social Security planning is a personal decision. If your situation is relatively straightforward, it might be unnecessary, but it could provide you with additional peace of mind if you are worried about making the right decisions.

Don't let a sense of pride hold you back. Outsourcing difficult or unpleasant work to people who make their living specializing in that area is something we do all our lives. It's just a way of managing your time and mental energy wisely.

If you feel like you can't hire a professional because of financial concerns, first see what you can do with the help of the Social Security Administration and trusted friends or relatives. If it turns out you have some questions that are just not clear, then consider whether the potential gain or loss from figuring that issue out is worth the investment with a professional. You may very well find that spending several hundred dollars right now could bring you many thousands in additional benefits in the years to come—a solid investment. In addition, a professional can help you look at all your options and make the best decision much more quickly than you could do on your own.

You'll feel better about your choice if you take the time to do some research and talk to several advisors before settling on one. Ask probing questions, and carefully consider their professional qualifications and affiliations and how they are paid. Even though there are plenty of unscrupulous people out there, don't let that cause you to be unreasonably suspicious of professionals who have worked hard to gain education and experience, and are charging reasonable compensation for their services.

You might feel like an expert by this point in the book! Or, at the very least, you're ready to stop learning about how Social Security works, get down to brass tacks, and get it done. In the next chapter, we'll look at how to combine everything into a workable plan to start your retirement journey.

CHAPTER NINE

BRINGING IT ALL TOGETHER AND FORMULATING YOUR PLAN

We've covered a lot of territory in this book. Your head might be spinning with all the information, wondering where to start. If so, this chapter is for you. We're going to bring it all together and get you started formulating your plan for Social Security in your retirement.

DECIDING WHETHER OR NOT TO DO IT YOURSELF

The first decision you need to make is whether to manage your Social Security decisions yourself using free online tools and services, or to enlist help by hiring a consultant or advisor.

When making this decision, remember that you want to do everything in your power to claim the benefits that are rightfully yours. While you can certainly try to make it a go on your own, a professional can be a big help. **Did you know that there are more than 80 ways a married couple could claim their Social Security benefits, depending on the chosen options?** A professional can help you sort through those options quickly to find the optimal one for you (source: https://PrepareforSocialSecurity.com/sources).

But no matter which direction you go, you will file for Social Security and, in all likelihood, receive benefits. Depending on when you file, your benefit amount will be different, but it is determined by how long you work, how much you earn while you work, and the age at which you file.

Doing the research, making the decisions, and filing on your own save you money in the short run. You don't have to pay any consultant or advisor fees, whether a percentage-based, hourly, or one-time fee. All the control is yours. If your situation is not complicated and you take the time to do your research well, you can come out with similar results as if you hired a professional.

On the other hand, handling Social Security on your own can mean losing out on money. **Only 4% of retirees claim Social Security at the optimal time. The 96% who don't lose an average of $111,000 per household—about $3.4 trillion in lost wealth** (source: https://PrepareforSocialSecurity.com/sources).

If you don't know exactly what you're doing when you retire and start claiming benefits, you can miss out on a lot of money without knowing it. This loss could be far more significant than anything you would conceivably have to pay a professional to get it done right in the first place.

Hiring a consultant can also ease your workload. You will still need to provide a significant amount of information to your consultant and make many of the final decisions yourself. No one else can make your Social Security decisions for you. However, you can appoint a representative who will have eFolder access to your documents through the Social Security Administration and can keep track of critical communications regarding your benefits.

If an advisor is willing to offer any of these services for free, you should take full advantage. Why would anyone give you free service? They may be selling other financial planning tools, insurance policies, or retirement investment plans that are their primary source of income. You may need to listen to a sales pitch, but you are under no obligation to purchase any other plans or services that you can't afford or are just not right for you. Offering complimentary Social Security advice is a way to get potential customers in the door.

DECIDING WHEN TO RETIRE

The next and most crucial decision you need to make is when to retire. You cannot claim Social Security retirement benefits before age 62. As we have seen, there are significant financial benefits to working past age 62 and preferably to your full retirement age before claiming benefits. In general, the longer you wait (up until age 70), the higher your benefits will be, increasing every month you push back retirement.

Claiming benefits at age 62 will give you 30% less in benefits every month for the rest of your life, and this can add up to thousands of dollars lost per year. If, on the other hand, you wait until age 70 to claim benefits, you will receive an extra 24% in your check every month. And so, you will have thousands of dollars more per year for a lifetime.

You will receive more checks throughout your retirement if you start drawing early. However, your total amount will likely be more significant if you wait until later to retire.

As you make this decision, consider your health and that of your spouse, as well as your family history. If you have severe health conditions or a family history that suggests your lifespan may not be as long as you'd like, this could be a reason to start drawing Social Security earlier.

HOW DOES SOCIAL SECURITY WORK IF YOU ALSO HAVE A PENSION THROUGH YOUR EMPLOYER?

An employer pension plan should not impact your Social Security benefits. If you paid into the Social Security system, you are entitled to your benefits regardless of what other kinds of investments or retirement savings you have accumulated over your lifetime.

If your pension is through a non-government employer and you paid FICA taxes, it should not affect your Social Security benefits. This will be the case for the vast majority of people. Most workers have FICA taxes or Federal Insurance Contributions Act taxes withheld from their paychecks as they are paid. Small business owners must pay the employer's and the employee's contribution amounts into the system. Those that do not will have reduced benefits as a result.

If your pension is through a non-government employer and you did not pay FICA taxes on it, that will impact your Social Security benefits. In this case, the Windfall Elimination Provision may apply to you. It covers people who earned pensions through such "non-covered" jobs but also qualify for Social Security from other jobs. This would generally apply if you worked for one or more employers that withheld Social Security taxes and one or more that did not.

There are restrictions on how much your benefits can be reduced (up to half and never to $0). Still, it is a special formula with many complicated elements. The formula takes into account your various forms of income, including the ones that did and did not pay into Social Security taxes during your career. This is something you will have to research for yourself on a case-by-case basis, but my professional recommendation is to use a Social Security consultant or advisor.

Finally, if you are the spouse, widow, or widower of someone who got a pension from a government job, you are affected by the Government Pension Offset, or GPO. If your government job did not pay Social Security taxes while you worked, your Social Security benefits would be reduced by two-thirds of your pension. This decrease is the GPO.

For instance, if your pension is $900 a month and your benefits are $1,000 a month, the GPO will be $600 (two-thirds of the pension), so you will only receive benefits of $400 a month, in addition to your $900 monthly pension. The GPO does not apply to all government workers; only to spouses, widows, and widowers with pensions from a federal, state, or local government job who did not pay Social Security taxes while the wage earner had the job.

Here are a few exceptions to the Windfall Elimination Provision and the Government Pension Offset.

These do not apply to you in the following situations:

- ✓ If you worked 30 years in jobs where you paid Social Security taxes.
- ✓ If you began working for the federal government after December 31, 1983.
- ✓ If your only pension is for working for a railroad.
- ✓ If you are a military reservist who receives a reservist pension.
- ✓ If you are a member of the clergy who receives a pension for their ministry.

JOINT LIFE EXPECTANCY

When making retirement decisions as a married couple, one thing to remember is that **joint life expectancy (the median age at the second spouse's death) is longer than the life expectancy of either individual.** For a 65-year-old individual, the IRS calculates life expectancy at 21 years. For a 65-year-old married couple, the joint life expectancy is 26.2 years. So the longer-living spouse would be expected to live to 91.

Considering that the surviving spouse may receive survivors benefits for the rest of their lives, such a long life expectancy is a good argument for taking Social Security as late as possible. This is especially true of the spouse with higher earnings.

SHOULD YOU USE THE BREAK-EVEN STRATEGY?

Your decision of when to file for Social Security will depend mainly on whether it's more important to you to maximize the money you receive in your lifetime, or the amount you get every month. Should you begin drawing Social Security checks earlier, giving you more checks during your lifetime with a smaller amount in each check? Or should you wait to file later, giving you larger monthly checks but fewer in your lifetime?

A break-even analysis shows how much your lifetime benefits will depend on which retirement date you pick to start drawing Social Security. If you die before reaching the break-even age, it's better to start collecting benefits earlier. If you live beyond it, waiting until later will be better for your bottom line. No one can predict the future. It will help you decide if you consider your family health history, including any current health problems, hereditary conditions, and the average longevity of people in your family.

Here are some steps to figuring out your break-even points using tools provided at www.ssa.gov/estimator:

- Find out your full retirement age.
- Figure out your full retirement benefit at that age.
- Determine your benefit at age 62.
- Determine how much you would receive in the 60 months between age 62 and your full retirement age at 67 if you start drawing your benefits at age 62.
- Figure out how many months you would have to live beyond 66 to break even.

If you are deciding between retiring at 62 rather than waiting until full retirement at 67, the break-even age is usually around 77 or 78. If you die earlier than that age, a break-even approach would say that taking the earlier retirement option would be beneficial. If you live longer than the break-even point, waiting until full retirement age to receive benefits would be better.

If you are deciding between retiring at 67 or delaying retirement until 70, the break-even age is usually a few months after your 82nd birthday. If you die earlier than 82, the break-even approach would favor starting your benefits at 67. On the other hand, if you live past that break-even point, it would be better for you to have waited until age 70 to retire.

There are some important caveats. The break-even strategy can be misleading, and it is not recommended by all advisors, certainly not in all situations. Some examples of problems with this strategy:

- If you include cost-of-living increases in Social Security in a break-even analysis, it can make it appear more beneficial than it really is to delay filing. Moreover, while COLA (cost-of-living-adjustment) increases averages by about 2.6%, it is not guaranteed. In some years, there is no COLA increase.

- The break-even strategy does not consider how much more money you could have earned had you taken Social Security earlier and invested the money in more profitable financial instruments. On the other hand, each year you wait to take benefits between your full retirement age and age 70, your benefits increase by 8%. This increase may not be as large as what you may earn in an excellent stock market year—it also comes with zero financial risk.

- A break-even approach might not make as much sense for a married couple as it would for an individual, especially in situations where your spouse may outlive you while drawing benefits based on your earnings record. If you accept lower monthly benefits, your spouse's benefits will be reduced as well. The life expectancy and financial needs of both spouses should be considered before making a decision.

It can be tempting to use the break-even point as a shortcut to give you the precise, optimal age you should claim benefits to get the best financial advantage. It doesn't work that way. Your situation, and that of your spouse, still require careful evaluation of a range of factors beyond those you type into a break-even calculator. Nonetheless, this tool can be one piece of the puzzle worthy of your consideration.

HOW CAN YOU SEE YOUR SOCIAL SECURITY STATEMENTS?

You can easily see your Social Security statements by logging into your "*my Social Security*" account or creating one if you haven't.

The process of creating one is straightforward. You will need a valid email address, cell phone number, and a government-issued ID, such as a driver's license or passport. You'll be prompted to input your information. At different times during the process, codes will be sent to your phone by text or voicemail that you will need to put into the online forms. You'll also need to upload a picture of yourself and the front and back of your ID.

If you are nearing retirement age (60 or older) but have not made a "*my Social Security*" account, the SSA will send you a Social Security statement annually, starting three months before your birthday. You can access your statements at https://www.ssa.gov/myaccount/statement.html. You can view them at any age; there is no need to wait until you are close to retirement age.

Your Social Security statement will contain several pieces of beneficial information:

- Retirement Benefits – whether or not you have enough credits to qualify for retirement benefits, as well as your full retirement age.
- Disability Benefits – how much you would receive per month if you became disabled right now.
- Survivors Benefits – how much your various family members would receive in benefits if you die.
- Personalized Monthly Retirement Benefit Estimates – showing your estimated benefit retiring each year (from 62 to 70 years old).
- Medicare – if you qualify for Medicare, and how to sign up.
- Earnings Record – how much of your earnings have been taxed for Social Security every year for the past 20 years (according to the sample statement).

- ✓ Earnings Not Covered by Social Security – a reminder that you may have some earnings, such as work for the government or a pension or retirement plan, that were not taxed for Social Security.
- ✓ A list of other important things to know about your Social Security benefits.

Your statement will also include a fact sheet based on your current age. You can also see the fact sheets anytime by going to https://www.ssa.gov/myaccount/statement.html.

WHERE DO WE GO FROM HERE?

In this chapter, we have walked through some of the main things you need to consider when formulating your plan for starting Social Security. Go back to previous chapters to refresh your memory and get more details on any steps that are still unclear.

There are a lot of unique situations we've not considered in this chapter, including divorced spouses, retirees with minor dependents, survivors benefits, various kinds of government workers, people with disabilities, and overseas claims. We'll consider all of those and more in Chapter 10.

CHAPTER TEN

SPECIAL SITUATIONS: DIVORCE, DISABILITY, CONTINUING TO WORK, AND MORE

In this final chapter, we will review some special situations, including divorced spouses, retirees with minor children, returning to work after retirement, survivors benefits for widows and widowers, government employees, the disabled, and overseas claiming.

While we don't have the space to go into each of these topics in detail, I would like to give you a basic overview to help you get started and know what to expect as you work out your Social Security in any of these circumstances.

HOW DOES SOCIAL SECURITY WORK FOR DIVORCED SPOUSES?

You can receive benefits based on your ex-spouse's work record under several conditions:

- ✓ You must have been married for at least ten years.
- ✓ You must currently be unmarried.

- ✓ Your ex-spouse must be 62 or older (the minimum age to claim Social Security).

- ✓ Your benefit based on your work must be less than your benefit based on your ex-spouse's work.

- ✓ You are entitled to Social Security benefits, either retirement or disability (you've met 20 credits in the 40-quarter period before becoming disabled).

Your benefits as a divorced spouse are 50% of what your ex-spouse will receive. The same calculations apply concerning waiting until your full retirement age to collect. Unlike average retirement benefits, your benefits based on an ex-spouse's work will not increase if you wait beyond your full retirement age. You do not need to wait until their full retirement age, as you can receive this even if your ex-spouse has not applied for retirement benefits yet. However, you must have been divorced for at least two years to collect benefits in this case.

You can also receive benefits based on their work even if they remarried. The benefits you receive based on your ex-spouse's work will have no impact on their benefits, nor would their benefits based on your work affect your benefits. The SSA will not even notify your ex-spouse that you are receiving benefits based on their work.

You will receive the highest benefit, which is based on your work or on your ex-spouse's work. You cannot receive both. For example, if your ex-spouse receives $3,000 a month in benefits, and you would receive $2,000 based on your own work, it would make more sense to take your own benefits. Your benefits based on your ex-spouse's work would only be $1,500 a month, as you receive 50% of their benefits.

On the other hand, if your benefits would be $1,200 based on your work, it makes sense to take the benefits as an ex-spouse. To clarify, receiving 50% of their benefits does not mean you are taking benefits from them. They will still receive 100% of their benefits, utterly unaffected by the fact that your benefits are based on their work record.

Some additional rules and conditions may apply, but these are the basics you need to know. Note that the earnings limit for retirement is also in place in this situation, so you'll need to stay below a specific monthly wage.

WHAT IF YOU HAVE MINOR DEPENDENTS WHEN YOU RETIRE?

Suppose you retire and still have minor children. In that case, your children can often collect Social Security benefits based on your work record and the benefits you claim. This benefit can also be applied to a grandchild who is legally dependent on you. To receive benefits, your dependent must be unmarried and under age 18. However, they can receive benefits through age 19 if they are a full-time high school student. If they have a disability that started before age 22, they can continue to receive benefits past age 18 with no age limit.

The benefits your dependent child receives will not decrease your retirement benefit. Your child will receive the equivalent of 50% of your Primary Insurance Amount (PIA), which is the benefit you would receive at full retirement age. If you earn $1,000 in benefits at full retirement age, your child will receive $500 in benefits, even if you don't wait until full retirement age.

However, your child cannot start receiving benefits until you file for benefits yourself. This means there are some circumstances in which it makes sense to retire before the full retirement age, based on the additional benefits your child would receive.

The SSA will pay a maximum family benefit to your immediate family based on your work record. Even if you, your wife, and two minor children can claim benefits based on your work record, the SSA will cap the total at somewhere between 150% to 180% of your benefits. You can see this formula on the "Formula for Family Maximum Benefit" page on the SSA's website. (All links mentioned in this chapter are available at https://PrepareforSocialSecurity.com/links.) However, you will likely want a professional to look more carefully at it. For example, if your benefit at full retirement age is $1,500, your maximum family benefit would be $2,484 based on the 2022 values.

A dependent child can only claim benefits on one parent's work record, even if both receive benefits. They will receive whatever the higher of the two benefits is. However, when at least one child qualifies on both parents' accounts, Social Security can combine the parents' family benefit maximums to free up a larger amount of benefits to be paid to the children. In this case, it will be up to you to determine which parent your child should claim benefits from, as the SSA will likely not automatically decide for you.

Dependent children are affected by the same earnings limits as you, in the case that they work while receiving benefits. You can see how that factors into their benefits by using the Retirement Earnings Test Calculator on the SSA's website.

WHAT IF YOU GO BACK TO WORK AFTER STARTING SOCIAL SECURITY?

Although we refer to the period of retirement as the "golden years," many people do not just want to sit around and do nothing. They want to continue working, not only to earn more income but also to feel a sense of purpose if they enjoy their work. But keep in mind that going back to work after starting Social Security only impacts you if you do so before your full retirement age. After you reach that age, your earnings will not affect your benefits.

If you want to keep working, you have two main options once you have started Social Security. The first is to receive benefits while working. If you have not reached retirement age and earn more than certain limits, at least $1 of your benefits will be withheld for every $2 you earn past the limit, which is currently around $20,000. This means your Social Security checks would be nonexistent for certain months, based on your expected earnings, and any overage that was withheld will be paid the following year.

If you reach full retirement age during a year, that limit is changed to over $50,000—a figure that changes each year. Keep in mind that $1 of your benefits will be withheld for every $3 over that earnings limit. This money that is withheld is not entirely lost. When you reach full retirement age, your benefits will be recalculated to account for the extra earnings while you have been receiving benefits.

The second option is to completely withdraw your application to receive benefits, which you can only do within 12 months of applying. You will have to pay back any benefits you have received, including what was withheld. You will be able to reapply later and receive a higher benefit. However, you are limited to one withdrawal per lifetime, so use it wisely.

Going this route is very messy, and you will not continue to receive benefits until you reapply or turn 70, whichever happens first. In effect, it is as if you never applied in the first place and are just continuing to build up your benefit for when you retire. If you are out of that 12-month window, you cannot withdraw. However, you can voluntarily suspend your benefits once you reach full retirement age. This will allow you to earn delayed retirement credits, increasing your eventual benefit.

A special rule is also applied to those who file for benefits in the middle of a year. In this case, they have potentially already earned more than the earnings limit of approximately $20,000. In that situation, you would receive a Social Security check for any whole month you are retired. The SSA defines these months as follows:

- If you are below full retirement age for a whole year, you are considered retired in any month that your earnings are approximately $1,630 or less, and you did not perform substantial services in self-employment.

- If you reach full retirement age during a year, you are considered retired in any month that your earnings are about $4,330 or less, and you did not perform substantial services in self-employment.

- Note that the dollar figures quoted here may change each year. For more up-to-date information, visit https://PrepareforSocialSecurity.com.

> To give one example, Craig retires before his full retirement age at the end of June, earning $37,000 up until that point for that year. At the beginning of October, he starts a business and makes $3,000 for the year while working 15 hours a week. He would receive Social Security checks for July, August, and September. Those were the only months in which his earnings were under the limit, and he was not substantially self-employed.

Given all this information, how should you think about working while drawing Social Security? Let's look at a few questions that get to the bottom line (source: https://PrepareforSocialSecurity.com/sources):

Is it a bad idea to keep working AND file for Social Security benefits? Many people headed for retirement are concerned about whether they can work after starting Social Security. Benefits may not be high enough to cover all living expenses after retirement, especially for those who do not have other retirement savings, workplace pensions, or 401(k)s.

The bottom line is yes, you can work while collecting Social Security benefits. However, if you are younger than full retirement age and make more than the yearly earnings limit set by the SSA, your benefits will be reduced until you reach full retirement age.

What income thresholds should you stay under? The income threshold is currently nearly $20,000 for a person who draws Social Security before reaching full retirement age. During the year that you reach full retirement age, the threshold is over $50,000.

This applies to wages from a job or net profit if you are in business for yourself. It includes bonuses, commissions, and vacation pay. You are not penalized for pensions, annuities, investment income, interest, veteran's benefits, or other government or military retirement benefits.

If you go over the income thresholds, what does that do to your Social Security benefits? For a person who is under full retirement age, benefit payments are reduced by $1 for each $2 you earn above the threshold.

When you reach full retirement age, the SSA will deduct $1 for each $3 you earn above the threshold. Beginning with the month you reach full retirement age, your earnings will not reduce your benefits no matter how much you make.

If you get penalized by Social Security for working after you claim, do you get those benefits back at some point, so it is not really a penalty? The SSA will recalculate your benefit amount and credit you for the months your benefits were reduced because of earnings that were higher than the SSA's earning limits for people drawing benefits.

WHAT IF YOUR SPOUSE HAS PASSED AWAY?

You cannot receive survivors benefits from your spouse as well as your benefits at the same time. The Social Security Administration will pay you the higher of the two. You cannot apply for survivors benefits online. You will need to call 1-800-772-1213 to request an appointment, or find your local SSA office and phone number at https://PrepareforSocialSecurity.com.

If you are the surviving spouse of someone eligible for Social Security, you can:

- Receive reduced benefits as early as age 60.
- Begin receiving benefits as early as 50 if you have a disability and the disability started within seven years of the worker's death.
- Receive survivors benefits at any age, if you have not remarried and you are the caregiver for the deceased worker's child who is under 16 or has a disability and receives child's benefits.

Each of these scenarios has a different percentage of the deceased worker's benefit amount that you will receive.

- A widow or widower at or above full retirement age—100%.
- A widow or widower aged 70—71.5% to 99%.

- A widow or widower aged 50 through 59, with a disability—71.5%.
- A widow or widower, any age, caring for a child under age 16—75%.

The maximum family amount will also affect these benefits, just like a spouse's or child's benefits would be. Your ability to claim benefits will also depend on whether or not and when you remarried. If you remarried before you turned 60 (or 50 if you are disabled), you would not be able to claim survivors benefits. If that marriage ends, you will regain eligibility for survivors benefits. If you remarry after 60, or 50 if you are disabled, your survivors benefits will be unaffected.

The SSA also provides answers to a few other situations:

- If you already receive benefits as a spouse, your benefit will automatically convert to survivors benefits after we receive the report of death.
- If you are also eligible for retirement benefits but haven't applied yet, you have an additional option. You can apply for retirement or survivors benefits now and switch to the other (higher) benefit later.
- For those already receiving retirement benefits, you can only apply for benefits as a widow or widower if the retirement benefit you receive is less than the benefits you would receive as a survivor.

For more information, see the article "Receiving Survivors Benefits Early" on the SSA website or at https://PrepareforSocialSecurity.com/links.

WHAT IF YOU ARE A GOVERNMENT EMPLOYEE OR RAILROAD WORKER?

If you worked at least ten years in the railroad industry (or five years after 1995), your benefits would be covered through the Railroad Retirement Board or RRB. This independent federal agency administers various employment benefits for railroad industry employees and their families.

These benefits are very similar to Social Security. For instance, the retirement calculations follow the same formula, based on the highest 35 years of earnings, with the same full retirement age and earliest age to be eligible for benefits. However, early retirement reductions do not apply if the worker has at least 30 years of RRB-covered employment. In that case, you can begin receiving benefits as early as age 60 with no age-based reduction.

There is also a second tier of retirement benefits, calculated in its own way, which resembles a comparable private defined benefit pension. You can find more information and apply at https://rrb.gov. If you worked on the railroad for less than ten years total or less than five years after 1995, your account is transferred to Social Security, and you will go through the SSA like most other workers.

The other main exception is federal government employees hired before 1984 whose jobs did not pay into Social Security. Those workers will be covered through the Civil Service Retirement System or CSRS. CSRS gives a lifetime annuity to civil servants after retirement based on their age, average salary, and years of service. You can find information and apply via the link on the Prepare for Social Security website, where you will learn more about eligibility and find forms to apply for retirement.

Other government workers may be covered by the Federal Employees Retirement System, or FERS, which replaced CSRS in 1987. Anyone hired after 1983 was automatically enrolled in FERS, and those enrolled in CSRS were allowed to change to the new system. FERS, unlike CSRS, provides benefits through Social Security, a basic benefit plan, and the thrift savings plan. Though the annuity is smaller than that offered by CSRS, these workers are eligible for Social Security, which can help supplement the annuity significantly. You can find information and apply at https://www.opm.gov/retirement-services/fers-information/, where you will learn more about eligibility and find forms to apply for retirement.

Certain state and local government employees may or may not be covered by Social Security. They may have a public pension instead of or in combination with Social Security. Either the Windfall Elimination Provision or the Government Pension Offset comes into effect in these situations.

HOW DOES HAVING A DISABILITY WHEN YOU RETIRE AFFECT YOUR SOCIAL SECURITY?

If you are eligible to receive multiple types of benefits (retirement and disability), the SSA will pay you only one—whichever is higher. Claiming early retirement may reduce your benefits from what you were receiving in disability. When you go on disability, you receive what you would get if you claimed benefits at full retirement age. This means that starting to take your early retirement will give you less money than you receive for your disability benefits. Once you reach your full retirement age, your benefits will automatically switch from disability. However, the amount should stay the same.

Some interesting cases arise. After claiming retirement benefits early, if you become disabled, you may be able to change to Social Security Disability Insurance. If you take early retirement but later find out that you might have qualified for a higher disability benefit, you may be able to claim it retroactively.

Your retirement benefit is based on your highest 35 years of income. If you become disabled, there is a chance you may have had much less time to work. In such cases, your SSDI benefit is determined by your inflation-adjusted average earnings from age 21 until the year you became disabled.

WHAT IF YOU LIVE OVERSEAS?

Residents of Cuba or North Korea are not able to receive payments. You will be able, however, to receive these payments if you move to a country where the Department of the Treasury is allowed to send payments. The United States has historically forbidden or placed restrictions on sending Social Security payments to the countries of the former Soviet Union, but the picture is not uniform. It is now permitted to receive payments in some of these countries with certain restrictions, and in some of them with no restrictions at all. Your best bet is to use the SSA's "Payments Abroad Screening Tool" available via https://prepareforsocialsecurity.com to find out what the current policy is for the country where you are planning to move.

Beyond that, the best resource about claiming Social Security overseas is the SSA resource "Your Payments While You Are Outside the USA." It explains how working abroad might affect your benefits, what information you need to provide, and how to report it.

There are different requirements depending on whether or not you are a U.S. citizen. If you are a U.S. citizen, you will need to report the following items:

- Any changes of address
- What work you complete outside the United States
- If, after claiming disability, you recover or return to work
- Marriage
- Divorce or annulment
- Adoption of a child
- A child leaves the care of a spouse or surviving spouse
- A child nearing 18 is a full-time student or disabled
- Death
- Inability to manage funds
- Deportation or removal to the United States
- If you are eligible for a pension from work not covered by Social Security

Benefits will be withheld the same way they would in the U.S. if you are receiving benefits yet continue to work and are younger than your full retirement age. You will receive a questionnaire periodically (every one or two years, depending on your age) to determine your continued eligibility for benefits.

Beyond that, the process is identical to living in the United States. You still need to file income taxes if you are a U.S. citizen, even if you live in a foreign country. You will still receive your benefits, calculated and paid in U.S. dollars, regardless of currency conversion rates.

CONGRATULATIONS, AND GOOD LUCK!

Now a word of congratulations is in order. Together, we've worked through a lot of complex issues related to Social Security. Don't worry if some of the information remains confusing. Feel free to go back and review as much as you need. Now that you know most of the ins and outs of Social Security planning for retirement, make sure to visit the Prepare for Social Security website and blog for even more in-depth information!

More importantly, you deserve congratulations for reaching the hard-earned milestone of retirement. You've worked hard for this, paid into the system consistently, and now you're ready to reap the rewards.

Please accept my personal invitation to visit https://TheMattFeretShow.com, which is my podcast and show. You can watch it on YouTube and listen to it on any podcast provider, including Apple Podcasts and Spotify.

I also encourage you to sign up for my FREE newsletter at https://PrepareforSocialSecurity.com or https://PrepareforMedicare.com. I send one or two emails a month, and the newsletter will help you stay up-to-date with your retirement, Social Security, and Medicare insurance coverage, as well as highlight timely news you can use and remind you about important dates throughout the year. When you sign up for the newsletter, you'll immediately get access to my helpful checklists for Social Security and Medicare. As always, access to the sites is free, as are the checklists.

Here's to your wealth, wisdom, and wellness!

—Matt Feret

ACKNOWLEDGEMENTS

Although my name is on the cover, you wouldn't be reading this book, nor would the website exist, without the contributions of a great number of personal and professional friends. Thank you for inspiring, encouraging, and supporting me many times over the year-plus it took this book and website to come to fruition. Thanks to the folks who graciously volunteered to be on my Advance Reader Team. You've provided extremely valuable feedback. It's truly heartwarming to be associated with you, and I sincerely thank you for being a part of my life.

A special note of thanks goes to Jim Blair, Marc Kiner, Joe D'Ambrose, Honorée Corder, Lucas Marino, LeiLani Whiteside, Kent Sanders, Paul Brown, Karen Hunsanger, Andrew Wood, and Dino Marino, all of whom helped me shape this book and the website.

As always, there's zero chance any of this exists without the love, support, and guidance provided by my wife, Niki. I love you.

GLOSSARY

62/70 split – a strategy in which the spouse with lower earnings begins drawing Social Security at age 62 while the higher-earning spouse waits to file for benefits at age 70.

401(k) – an employer-sponsored retirement account in which employers may match employee contributions.

AIME – Average Indexed Monthly Earnings

Appeals Council – a body of the SSA that considers the cases of Social Security applicants who do not agree with the SSA's decision about their benefits eligibility or amount.

Average Indexed Monthly Earnings – an average of your earnings for your 35 highest-earning years of work, with zeros for each year less than 35 you worked. This figure is used to determine your monthly Social Security retirement benefit.

Break-even age – the age when the dollar value of claiming benefits later equals the value of taking them early.

GLOSSARY

Certified Financial Planner (CFP) – This is a recognized expert in financial planning, taxes, insurance, estate planning, and retirement. A CFP has higher education in their field, has passed standardized exams, and has demonstrated experience and ethical integrity. They also have a fiduciary duty, which means they must make decisions with the client's best interests in mind.

Chartered Retirement Planning Counselor (CRPC) – This professional concentrates on helping clients work through retirement-related problems. They must complete six courses before receiving the CRPC designation and complete 16 hours of continuing education every two years.

Chartered Retirement Plans Specialist (CRPS) – This professional develops and manages retirement plans for businesses. They are required to complete 16 hours of continuing education every two years to maintain their status.

COLA – Cost of Living Adjustment

Cost of living adjustment – an increase in the amount of Social Security benefits, based on an index of the price of consumer goods. Benefits are not always increased every year.

Credits – the system used by the SSA to determine retirement benefit amounts. Credits are based on a worker's earnings. Four can be earned in a year, and 40 are necessary to receive full benefits.

Double-whammy effect – refers to the fact that some Social Security benefits are subject to taxation.

Fiduciary obligation – a legal responsibility of certain financial professionals to act in the client's best interests, even if they receive less money for doing so.

File and suspend – a strategy of filing for benefits in which the higher-earning spouse files for benefits at full retirement age and immediately suspends them. The lower-earning spouse collects a spousal benefit, while the higher-earning partner waits to draw benefits at age 70.

Full retirement age – the age at which you are entitled to receive your full retirement benefit (rather than the reduced amount you receive if you retire earlier). This number depends on the year you were born.

Government Pension Offset – a government policy in which, if you receive a retirement or disability pension from a federal, state, or local government based on your own work for which you didn't pay Social Security taxes, the SSA may reduce the Social Security benefits for a spouse, widow, or widower.

"Hold harmless rule" – a government policy that does not permit increases in Medicare premiums to lower monthly Social Security checks. This rule applies only to people who deduct their Medicare premiums from their Social Security checks, not to those who pay their premiums directly.

ICEP – Initial Coverage Election Period. This only matters if you defer signing up for Medicare Part B for some reason, such as working past age 65 and maintaining employer-based health insurance coverage during that time. The ICEP is your first opportunity to choose a Medicare Advantage plan instead of Original Medicare. When you join Medicare Part B later, your ICEP is the three months before your Part B coverage takes effect. If you enroll in Part B when you turn 65, your ICEP is the same as your IEP.

IEP – the Initial Enrollment Period. When you're first eligible for Medicare, you have a seven-month Initial Enrollment Period to sign up for Part A and/or Part B. If you're eligible for Medicare when you turn 65, you can sign up during the three months before the month you turn 65, the month you turn 65, and the three months after you turn 65.

Joint life expectancy – for a married couple, the median age of the second spouse's death. Joint life expectancy is longer than the life expectancy of either individual.

GLOSSARY

Maximum taxable earnings – the maximum amount you can earn from work each year while drawing Social Security without reducing the amount of your Social Security benefits. This amount is adjusted by the government each year.

Medicare – Federal health insurance for people over age 65. Also available for certain people with disabilities who are under age sixty-five and have ESRD or ALS.

Medicare Part A – hospital insurance; covers inpatient hospital care, skilled nursing facility, hospice, surgery, and home healthcare.

Medicare Part B – helps pay for services from doctors and other health care providers, lab tests, outpatient care, home healthcare, and durable medical equipment.

Medicare Part C – also known as Medicare Advantage. These are "combo" products of Medicare Parts A, B, and D. There is no "public" option Medicare Part C offering; all are sold by authorized Medicare insurance companies. Commonly referred to by the acronym MAPD, which stands for Medicare Advantage Prescription Drug. Less commonly used or known, but can also refer to MA-only plans, DSNP plans, or SNP plans.

Medicare Part D – Also referred to as a PDP, a Part D Plan, or a Medicare Part D Prescription Drug Plan. These are stand-alone Prescription Drug Plans and do not cover any medical procedures—they only cover prescription drugs. Medicare Part D is also the Prescription Drug 'PD' in an MAPD plan. There are no "public option" Medicare Part D Prescription Drug Plans, and these are only sold by authorized Medicare insurance companies.

Medicare Supplement (also known as Medigap) – There are no "public option" Medicare Supplement plans—they are only sold by authorized Medicare insurance companies. These policies help fill "gaps" in Original Medicare. Plans are standardized by letters. The most popular and comprehensive plans are Plan F and Plan C (if eligible for Medicare prior to 1/1/2020) or Plan G and Plan N.

Medicare Supplement Open Enrollment Period – automatically starts the month you're 65 and enrolled in Medicare Part B. If you defer Medicare Part B because, for example, you're working and have employer-sponsored healthcare coverage, the period starts when you finally do elect Medicare Part B. This is a one-time, six-month enrollment window. After this period, you may not be able to buy a Medicare Supplement policy without answering health questions. If you're able to buy one, it may cost more due to past or present health problems.

Original Medicare – refers to Medicare Parts A and B only.

PIA – Primary Insurance Amount

Primary Insurance Amount – your Social Security benefit at full retirement age.

Railroad Retirement Board – an independent federal agency that administers benefits for railroad employees and their families. Participants are not eligible for Social Security benefits.

Retirement Income Certified Professional (RICP) – This is an expert in retirement income planning. To earn this designation, they must have three years of business experience and complete three courses with exams.

Social Security – a social insurance program funded by workers and employers, designed to partially replace earnings lost to retirement, disability, or death for workers and their families.

Social Security Act – the law establishing the Social Security System, signed by President Franklin D. Roosevelt in 1935.

Social Security Administration – the federal agency that administers Social Security.

Social Security Disability Insurance – a payroll tax-funded federal insurance program that provides monthly benefits to people who have a medical disability that restricts their ability to work.

Social Security Trust Funds – two accounts used by the U.S. government to receive payroll taxes and pay out benefits to retirees, disabled workers, and survivors. Surplus receipts are invested in low-risk, interest-earning U.S. government securities.

Split strategy – a strategy in which a husband and wife claim Social Security benefits at different ages to maximize their total benefit or to meet other financial priorities.

SSA – Social Security Administration

ssa.gov – website of the Social Security Administration

SSDI – Social Security Disability Insurance

SSI – Supplemental Security Income

Supplemental Security Income – a program that provides cash payments to disabled children, disabled adults, and people aged 65 or older.

Survivors benefits – benefits paid to widows, widowers, and dependents of eligible workers.

Windfall Elimination Provision – a formula used to adjust Social Security benefits for people who receive non-covered pensions and qualify for Social Security based on other Social Security-covered earnings.

WHO IS MATT FERET?

Matt Feret began his professional career in live television news reporting and anchoring in and around rural Virginia, Missouri, Kentucky, and Illinois before going back to graduate school. While in school, he got a customer service job at the local Blue Cross and Blue Shield to help pay for tuition. It was there that he discovered his passion for directly and personally helping people navigate the healthcare and retirement maze.

He's made professional stops at Elevance Health, Humana, HCSC, CVS Health/Aetna. The thoughts and opinions expressed in this publication are those of the author only and are not the thoughts and opinions of any current or former employer of the author. Nor is this publication made by, on behalf of, or endorsed or approved by any current or former employer of the author.

Matt really loves his wife and kids who tolerate living with him in a suburb of Chicago. The family also includes a cat, Puck, who was apparently named after a Shakespeare character. His kids made him add Puck's name to this bio.

Matt loves public and private speaking—come connect with him on the interwebs!

Company Name:
　MF Media, LLC

Email:
　mf@mattferet.com

Websites:
　https://PrepareforMedicare.com

　https://PrepareforSocialSecurity.com

　https://PrepareforPassing.com

　https://TheMattFeretShow.com

LinkedIn:
　linkedin.com/in/mattferet

Facebook:
　https://www.facebook.com/PrepareforMedicare

　https://www.facebook.com/PrepareforSS

Twitter:
　@feret_matt

More Books by Matt Feret:
　https://www.amazon.com/author/mattferet

INDEX

401(k) 2, 33, 60, 138
62/70 split 30, 138

A

Adopted 13, 35, 48
Adoption 135
Adoptive 36
AIME 17, 138
Annual statement 28–29
Appeal 15–16, 27, 40, 42, 61, 100–102, 104, 106, 108–109, 111, 138
Appeals Council 15, 101, 138
Application 14–16, 30–31, 35, 40–41, 93–95, 105, 129
Attorney/Lawyer ix, 41-42, 53-56, 61, 101, 104, 108–109, 111
Average Indexed Monthly Earnings 17, 138

B

Beneficiary 34, 50, 80

Benefits ii–viii, x–xiv, xvi, 1–44, 46–54, 57–67, 73–74, 77, 79–84, 86–89, 91–93, 95–100, 104–108, 110–111, 114–135, 138–143

Break-even age 24–26, 121, 138

C

Calculators xiii–xiv, 16, 24, 27, 29, 38–39, 61, 86, 91–93, 99, 103, 106, 109, 122, 128

Case studies vi, xii, 43

Certified Financial Planner (CFP) 112, 139

Chartered Retirement Planning Counselor (CRPC) 113, 139

Chartered Retirement Plans Specialist (CRPS) 112, 139

Children iv, vi, xii, xvi, 1–2, 6–7, 11–14, 31, 35, 57, 59, 63, 65–66, 94, 125, 127–128, 143

Clergy 52, 59, 120

Cost of living adjustment (COLA) 3, 29, 122, 139

Congress 5–7, 10–11, 20, 32, 102

Credits xi, 12–13, 16, 34, 51–52, 59, 83, 92, 95, 123, 126, 129, 139

D

Dependents, ii, xi–xii, 2, 5-6, 8, 13, 21, 26, 36, 80, 104-105, 124, 127-128, 143

Disability ii, iv, xi, xv–xvi, 2, 5–7, 12–14, 31, 34–36, 38, 40–41, 46–48, 54, 59, 64, 66, 76, 80, 83, 85, 102–103, 109, 111, 114, 123–127, 131–132, 134–135, 140–143

Divorce 9, 30–32, 64–66, 94, 105, 125

Divorced xv, 4, 9, 31–32, 35, 46–48, 59, 64–65, 105, 124–126

Documents 14, 40–41, 74, 94, 96, 105, 113, 117

Double-whammy effect 139

E

Earnings limits 39, 128

Enroll x–xi, xiii, 41, 85–86, 95, 140

Enrollment 37, 80, 82, 85, 88, 140, 142

Exemptions 36–37

F

Federal workers 59

Fiduciary obligation 139

Field office 5

File v, x–xi, 10, 14–16, 22, 24, 30, 32, 39, 50, 54, 58, 62, 64, 66, 76, 85–86, 88, 91, 96–97, 100–101, 104–105, 113, 117, 120–121, 127, 129–130, 138–139

File and suspend 10, 139

Filing xiv, 9–10, 16, 27, 33, 37, 47, 56, 58–59, 64–65, 76, 82, 85–86, 91, 93, 95, 97, 104, 107, 109, 114, 117, 122, 139

Financial advisor vii–viii, 69, 72, 114

Full retirement age 2, 9–10, 14, 16–19, 23, 25, 29–32, 36, 38–39, 44, 46–47, 49–50, 62–63, 80, 82, 92, 118, 121–123, 126–131, 133–135, 139–140, 142

G

Government employees 125, 133

Government Pension Offset 119, 133, 140

Grandchildren 2, 11, 13, 35, 65

H

Health 3, 7–8, 12, 14, 23–24, 26–28, 38, 41, 47, 62, 84–85, 89, 118, 121, 140–142, 144

Hold harmless rule 81, 140

I

Immigrants 11, 59

Inflation iii, 3, 5, 9, 16–17, 28–29, 33, 38, 49, 92, 97, 134

International exemptions 37

J

Joint life expectancy 120, 140

L

Life expectancy 1, 8, 14, 27–28, 30, 38, 42, 120, 122, 140

Lifespan 2, 7, 24, 26–27, 47, 62, 90, 118

Lump sum 9, 14–15, 34, 62–63

M

Married, iii–iv, xii, 4, 9, 22, 27, 30–36, 43–44, 48, 62, 64-65, 76, 94, 97, 105, 107, 116, 120, 122, 125, 132, 135

Maximum taxable earnings 19, 141

Medicare i, iv, vi–viii, xii–xv, 7, 29, 63, 69–70, 76–77, 79–91, 95, 99, 103, 123, 136, 140–142

Medicare Part A 81, 83, 85, 88–89, 141

Medicare Part B 29, 63, 81, 83, 85–86, 89, 140–142

Medicare Part C 89, 141

Medicare Part D vii–viii, xiv, 81–82, 84–85, 87–89, 141

Military xv, 6, 10, 19, 39–40, 69, 95–96, 120, 130

O

Overseas, 88, 124–125, 134

P

Pension ii, vi, 2, 10, 19, 21, 26, 38–39, 64, 83, 85, 96, 118–120, 124, 130, 133, 135, 140, 143

PIA, 17, 127, 142

Prescription drugs 80, 84, 89, 141

Primary Insurance Amount 17, 127, 142

R

Railroad 52, 59, 83, 85, 95, 120, 132–133, 142

Railroad Retirement Board 52, 83, 85, 132, 142

Religious exemptions 36

Remarriage 31, 34–35, 48

Representative, 15–16, 41, 53–54, 60–61, 63, 101, 104, 117

Retirement Income Certified Professional (RICP) 112, 142

Retirement plan xiii–xiv, 3, 112, 124, 139, 147

Roth IRA 33

S

Scams 73, 75, 77

Self-employment 34, 52, 96–97, 129

Social Security i–xvi, 1–62, 64–66, 68–86, 88, 90–136, 138–143

Social Security Act 6, 142

Social Security Administration iii–iv, xvi, 1, 5, 10, 12–18, 23, 27–28, 41, 43, 45, 49–50, 52–53, 58, 61, 69–74, 80, 86, 93, 100, 107, 115, 117, 131, 142–143

Social Security Card 70, 73

Social Security Disability Insurance 12, 134, 143

Social Security Statement 70, 95, 123

Social Security Trust Fund 20, 32, 143

Split strategy 44, 143

Spousal benefit 10, 30–32, 44, 46, 139

SSA iii–iv, x, xiv, 5, 13, 15–19, 28–30, 32, 34, 38–42, 45–46, 50–51, 53–56, 60–61, 63, 69, 71–76, 81, 86, 91–106, 108–109, 121, 123–124, 126–134, 138–140, 143

ssa.gov xiv, 5, 39, 69, 71–72, 75, 86, 94, 99, 121, 123–124, 143

SSDI 12, 134, 143

SSI 12, 103, 143

Statement 28–29, 40, 70, 95, 104, 123–124

Stepchildren 13, 35

Student exemptions 37

Supplemental Security Income 12, 95, 143

Survivors benefits xii, 2, 13–14, 18, 31, 34–36, 40, 46–48, 51, 64, 80, 104–105, 120, 123–125, 131–132, 143

T

Taxes 4, 7, 9, 11, 20–21, 31, 33, 36–37, 44, 51–52, 58–59, 80–81, 83, 92, 97–99, 104, 112, 118–120, 135, 139–140, 143

W

Website i, vii, ix–x, xiii–xiv, 5, 12–13, 15, 28, 34, 38, 40–41, 53–54, 61, 69–73, 76, 78–81, 85–86, 91, 93, 99, 103, 109–114, 127–128, 132, 136–137, 143, 145

When to claim xi, 22–23

Widow 2, 13, 18, 31, 34–35, 46, 104–105, 119, 125, 131–132, 140, 143

Widower 6, 13, 18, 31, 34–35, 48, 104–105, 119, 125, 131–132, 140, 143

Windfall Elimination Provision 119, 133, 143

Withholding 29, 82

Work history 12, 31–32

Working iv, xi–xii, 2, 4–6, 9, 12–13, 19, 23–24, 30–31, 37–39, 42, 44, 47–51, 58, 60, 78, 98, 102, 107, 118, 120, 128, 130–131, 134, 140, 142

Made in United States
Troutdale, OR
01/29/2024